Ghostly Tales
of
Tasmania

by

Joan Dehle Emberg

and

Buck Thor Emberg

ISBN 0 949457 44 2

24 Wellington Street, Launceston, Tasmania
Telephone (03) 6331 4222
sales@regalpress.com.au
www.regalpress.com.au

ACKNOWLEDGEMENTS

The authors were expecting to be able thank all the people who helped with this volume of 'Ghostly Tales of Tasmania'.

Unfortunately, there are so many scores of contributors that the task has become impossible. We CAN acknowledge the fact that not once did we receive anything except gracious help, and we have the added bonus of having made many new friends.

We look forward to having many more cups of tea with all of you who have helped.

We do wish to publicly acknowledge the help of local Launceston historian, Dennis Hodgkinson, who contributed six stories from the Launceston area.

Thank you, one and all.

INTRODUCTION

Not unlike Ireland, Tasmania is one of those fortunate places which still has an oral tradition. Families still enjoy sitting around the fire and telling stories. Many of these stories have been handed down through the generations. We are fortunate – and somewhat unique in the Western World – in the sense that we haven't entirely given in to the electronic media: we haven't left all the storytelling to radio and television.

Although Tasmania is as modern as most other parts of the world, we have fortunately been able to retain something of the 'old world'. We are still a family-oriented society, and stories are easily shared from home to home. Our small population is also a help in maintaining this oral tradition.

A wise man once said, "There are no secrets in Tasmania." This is fairly true. Some would call the passing on of secrets 'gossip'. We prefer the term 'oral tradition', and for this tradition we are indeed fortunate. The result is a deep and unique knowledge of ourselves both as individuals and as a society...and a local knowledge found in few parts of the industrial/electronic world.

The same wise man also observed that Tasmanians speak of teachers, not education; they talk about doctors, not medicine; they discuss politicians, not politics. Could anything be closer to the truth? We think not. We also think this is a further indication of how close we are to ourselves as a society.

The above characteristics make for a warmer, friendlier, and some-times nosier Tasmania; and it has been these qualities which have made the writing of this book so much fun.

During the mid '70's, when we began our graveyard studies (which led to the publication of 'Gravely Tasmanian' Vols. I, II & III, now retitled 'Living Stones' Vols. I, II & III), we quickly became aware that many people also had ghost tales to tell. "One day," we said.

So, here we present for your enjoyment Volume I of GHOSTLY TALES OF TASMANIA. There will be at least one more volume, perhaps two.

We have, at all points, been as 'scientific' as possible, even though 'science' seems to have little to do with ghost tales. By 'scientific', we mean that we have related the stories as told to us as accurately as we could. We have not added to or varnished stories beyond adding some dramatization at certain key spots. In short, the facts of the stories are as they were told to us (or as close as we could make them).

Neither did we approach this study with a bias that ghosts do or do not exist. We are not ghostbusters trying to prove or disprove the phenomena described in the stories. Nor are we exorcists.

This book is simply a collection of tales told to us by Tasmanians.

Having heard so many tales and written so many stories, have we come to believe in the supernatural? This is a question people frequently ask. Our answer is almost bureaucratic: 'well, yes and no'. What does one believe when one's very expensive electronic camera will not set up to take pictures during the very spooky Port Arthur Ghost Tour? This happened to the authors, not once, not twice, but THREE times, twice in the Model Prison, and once at the Parson's House. Was it just a coincidence that our torch also refused to work, yet it worked perfectly both before and after the tour? Incidentally, the same camera acted 'funny' when we were trying to take shots of the cellar of Prospect House, the alleged 'haunt' of Mrs. Buscombe.

And how can we account for the very real and physical difficulty we both experienced in passing through the doorway at Mauriston House, except to say that something we could neither see nor hear had presented a barrier? Neither of us were in the least aware that the same difficulty had been experienced by others.

And how can one account for the curious and seemingly unexplainable phenomena experienced by successive generations...the repeated appearances of Mrs. Buscombe at Prospect House, or the curious smell at Brickenden?

Although we don't 'believe' in all ghostly phenomena, we have come to believe that some of these phenomena need more than chemistry or physics to understand their cause.

This book is presented to the reader with no specific attitude about ghosts or ghouls or creaking stairs. We leave that to fertile imaginations...after all, that's half the fun.

We can say that every story in this volume, and all pictures, are a direct result of our research. Some of the incidents happened to us;

most were related by other people. We do NOT guarantee their veracity. How can we?

It is ALWAYS impossible to be totally accurate when doing social research. Field notes might be unfortunately sketchy. It is entirely possible (and understandable) for one or two of our contributors to claim, 'but that's not what I said!' If this is the case, help us correct the errors...and please tell us more ghostly tales for Volume II. Let us know, and we'll drop by for a chat, and a cuppa...and a tale or two.

Most of all, have fun with the tales in this Volume. We know that you will be both amused and bemused...and sometimes even thrilled or scared (we hope!).

August, 1990
Golconda, Tasmania

Contents

Acknowledgements	iii
Introduction	v
The Ghost Who Hated A Closed Front Door	1
The Black Cat	3
The Horrifying Presence Of Parliament House	5
The Blue Lady Of The Old Royal Hobart Hospital	7
The Young Girl At Pontville	8
Madman's Hill	9
A Poltergeist	10
St. John's Park	11
The Murdered Stockman And The Old Kempton Inn	13
Old Artie	14
Mauriston House At The Hunting Ground	16
Kodak Headquarters, Hobart	20
Animal Ghosts	23
The Bicycle Ghost Of St. Helen's	24
Goulds Country ... You Can Feel The Haunting	26
Mystery Lady Of Pyengana	30
The 'Double Ghost' Of Pyengana	32
The Golconda Ghosts	34
The Three Sailers Of Four Mile Creek	37
The Light In The Brewery Window	40
Ghostly Corner Of The Blue Tiers	43
Bushwalkers' Ghost	45
The Murdered Barmaid Of Salamanca Place	47
The Bare Bones Of Fred At The Royal	49

Blood At Bona Vista	51
Leg Irons At Wesley Dale	53
Garth	54
They Call Her Guinevere	58
The Swallowed Gold Sovereign	60
Many Happenings At St. Andrew's Inn	62
Norwich House, Norfolk Plains	64
The Light In The Mirror	68
The Ghostly Smell Of Brickendon	69
Ghostly Bikies!	70
The Hallway	73
The Man With Four Daughters	77
The Ghost Of The Ball And Chain	80
Old Wrest Point Staircase	81
The Mornful Music Of Wanstead	82
The Flogging Ghost Of Richmond Bridge	84
The Drunken Hag Of Campbell Town	85
The Haunted Road	86
John Batman's Ghost?	88
"A Quarter Past Eleven"	89
The Swinging Door Of Valley Field	90
The Strangled Dog Of Sassafras	91
Bothwell's Grey Lady	92
A Chinese Ghost	93
William Rumney Never Did Want To Leave Home	94
The Ghost Of Gibbet Hill	95
The Phantom Of The Princess Theatre	97
Mr. Ellis' Friendly Ghost	99
The Restless Soul Of Penquite or The Case Of The Footless Tracks	100
The Haunted Cell	102
Calumet	103
The Ghost Of Mrs. Buscombe	104

Gunshots And Blue Smoke At Sherwin 107
The Ghosts Of Entally House 109
Ratteskellar 112
The Lovely Lady Of Richmond Gaol 114
A Lady's Ghost - Or A Guardian Angel? 115
Ghostly Port Arthur 117
The Model Prison 119
The Parson's House 122
The Commandant's House 124
The Powder Magazine 126

THE GHOST WHO HATED A CLOSED FRONT DOOR

Lena Hefford lives a very simple life in the shadow of the mountains north of Avoca. Lena has ALWAYS lived an uncomplicated life at or near 'Broomsgrove'. She is not the sort of person who gives her mind to things she doesn't know or understand.

Now a healthy eighty year-old (despite a recent set back), Lena still lives an active life. Keith, her son and manager of 'Broomsgrove', has the same practical bent of spirit. But this is Lena's story.

During a period in her lifelong farming career, Lena moved to the old farmhouse, 'Melrose'. This old homestead (c.1840) is close to 'Garth' and at the end of a seldom-used road. The family's occupation of 'Melrose' was to be short-term, as they were in the process of buying their own farm.

Each day would go pretty well as the day before: work, eat, work, maybe the wireless, and an early bedtime. Then, of course, the inevitable early rising as befits the simple life. This was a continuing, daily cycle.

There was also another part of that cycle...a repeated 'happening' which took place at precisely 8.00 each night. The 'happening' continued for the entire year of the family's residence: the front door would open...every night...at exactly at 8:00 p.m.

"It didn't really bother us," Lena claims. "Nothing happened. Only the door opened. Nothing else. It happened when my brother Bill was visiting. He thought it was someone dropping in for a cup of tea. We all just sort of smiled. It was 8:00 o'clock, and we knew what it was...the door had opened. After all, it WAS 8:00 o'clock. Bill believed us after that."

Members of the family still puzzle over the door that wanted to be open. Not Lena, though. For her, it was merely a presence of some kind which 'sort of' liked to open the front door...at precisely the same time...EACH night. It didn't effect their work, so what was there to worry about?

Maybe the ghost who hates a closed front door still visits 'Melrose'. If so, no one would know – the house has been empty for years. And

1

the hunters who use the old house as an occasional shack keep the front door tightly...LOCKED.

If you have a door which mysteriously opens, perhaps the ghost of 'Melrose' has migrated to your house. Don't worry...It's friendly.

The Ghostly Smell of Brickenden
Brickenden, Longford.

The Ghost who Hated a Closed Front Door
Melrose, Fingal Valley.

THE BLACK CAT

Why black cats? Why midnight? Why bumps in the night? Why footsteps up the stairs? Why glowing lights? Why grey ladies standing at the foot of beds? We don't even know how to make guesses in answer to such questions. The more tales of Tasmanian ghosts we are told, the less we comprehend.

We don't understand the story of the Black Cat either. Once more, the people who tell the tale are normal, hard working folk with no discernible difference from the rest of Tasmanians.

But they DID have a cat!

Karley brought home a black kitten. It was a cute kitten which easily followed the young girl. They were instant loves for each other. Mother, of course, said, "No, you cannot keep it." Then she relented. She does remember, however, that she did not like the cat. Karley and the rest of the children in the family also learned to dislike, then hate, then fear, the animal. The Black Cat was driven by something inside which none of the family could comprehend.

As the kitten grew into cathood, it developed strange behaviour patterns. For instance, the cat would hide on the refrigerator or on top of the furniture and leap at the children's throats, sometimes scratching them badly. It seemed as if the cat was possessed by 'something'. Mother said that it became a battle of wills, with the cat staring and attacking...and always winning. Mother and the cat hated each other.

Well, we must ask, why did they not get rid of the cat? That seemed to be the thing they should have done. But battles of wills are difficult to explain. Perhaps both drew strength from each other. In other words, the cat stayed.

One day, friends Nick and Tracey visited the family. They, too, took an instant dislike to the cat. "Get rid of it," they said. "There's something evil about that cat!" They knew nothing about the animal, except to say that it seemed to be thinking evil...and plotting harm.

Not only Nick and Tracey, but other friends and visitors began noticing strange things about the cat. Nor had they been prompted to say so. The negative feeling about Black Cat grew.

3

Perhaps it was because the slits in the cat's pupils were horizontal and not vertical...like other cats. Maybe that is what caused the feelings of doom and foreboding! A cat with horizontal pupils? Yes. It was if its very eyes were an omen of something not good.

Mother said the house became cold at times when the cat was around. And it seemed bent on destroying her soul as it stared unceasingly at her from its many lairs. Was it going to attack? Or was it going to purr?

The Black Cat was not only dangerous to children and adults. Black Cat also attacked dogs. One such animal was the local Great Dane whose nose it tore open in a frenzy of fury. The dog was terrified and fled from the cat's presence. Black Cat drove away and/or killed other family cats. The favourite family cat died of an apparent heart attack...found, if it is possible, 'cat scared'.

One day, the family received a phone call. Black Cat had been to a neighbour's farm and had killed their goats! Goats? Yes, goats! 'Not possible,' you say? Black Cat was observed killing goats! It was fearless and would attack anything...no provocation was needed. Black Cat respected no one and nothing. It was totally fearless.

Black Cat sat on the fridge and watched, and waited...and waited...and watched. The whole family was afraid of it; even the father of the family was cowed by its behaviour. He dealt with the 'thing' by leaving it alone and giving it a wide berth. He could always go to work.

What did the family do? Finally, they moved; and, happily, Black Cat did not follow them. The tale is over. Or is it?

If you ever see a Black Cat with pupils that are horizontal instead of vertical, watch out! There's a very strong chance that it might ATTACK!

THE HORRIFYING PRESENCE OF PARLIAMENT HOUSE

There are some parts of Parliament House which SHOULD be haunted. Many things have happened through the course of its history which could well provide a ghost. And there are parts of it which FEEL haunted. A visit to the undercroft (which now houses a museum) is proof enough of this. Perhaps it is the cold stone walls...perhaps it is the shadows formed by the vaulted ceiling...perhaps it is an echo from the corridor. Yet there are those who swear the 'it' is a mysterious figure who walks silently in the shadowy recesses and who, upon discovery, quickly disappears. Some wags say that it may be an elusive politician!

But the door to the Speaker's Room looks anything but haunted. As one walks up the stairs from the reception area and turns along the corridor, one receives a feeling of day-to-day business. The carpet, white walls, and wood panelling don't seem to encourage ghosts. Yet there are those who swear they have experienced a 'horrifying presence'.

The people who have reported the presence are those who work late at night when the building is empty. Felicity was one of those people. As a cleaner, she was responsible for the Speaker's Room. She was also a strong-minded woman and not easily intimidated. Yet many a time she had to be rescued by husband Clarrie because she had 'frozen' to the spot, right in the doorway, unable to move. Clarrie describes her as being rigid, her eyes staring, her hair standing up on the back of her neck.

Others have independently told the same story. Mary was unable to pass through the doorway. Something made her stop...a horrifying 'something'...and wouldn't let her proceed. Mitch reported a similar experience as he started work in the small grey hours of early morning.

Many years ago, a policeman told the authors that rookie cops were not sent to Parliament House for nighttime duty. Was he kidding?

Over-stimulated imaginations? A real manifestation of draughts in an empty building? The legacy of some tragic happening in times past? No matter what, there are those who testify to the horrifying presence of Parliament House...right at the Speaker's door.

The Horrifying Presence of Parliament House
The Undercroft.

The Horrifying Presence of Parliament House
Speaker's Door.

THE BLUE LADY OF THE OLD ROYAL HOBART HOSPITAL

A nurse friend of ours who has left nursing for a time to finish raising her family tells the story of the 'Blue Lady'. For years this apparition has appeared to a number of workers in the hospital. But you need not worry if you find yourself in the Royal Hospital. The Blue Lady is, indeed, a person who will not harm anyone. Instead, she is a symbol of help.

The story, as it is recorded, is about how, on some evenings, a nursing sister will appear in private rooms or sometimes in wards. She has a look of deep concern as she stands at the end or side of the bed. She never speaks, but neither does she unnerve the patient. Rather, patients have said that her presence was deeply comforting.

How do we know that it was not merely a nursing sister on her rounds? The Blue Lady has a slight glow to her, and she has been seen and described as an older woman when there were NO older nurses on duty in that part of the hospital. The Blue Lady is also always concerned with the welfare of the patients who have described her.

Sometimes there is a hazy blue light coming from wards in the deep of the night: the same nights when the Blue Lady has appeared to patients.

If you see her, count it as a blessing.

THE YOUNG GIRL AT PONTVILLE

Marion and Peter own the home now, but the young girl sometimes still sits at the head of the stairs in the old homestead. For many decades she has been seen by people from diverse parts of Australia...even generations it is said.

What does she do? Actually, nothing of particular interest except that she sits at the top of the stairs in the same clothes in which she allegedly died.

It would seem that she is sad as she sits there on the stairs looking wistfully out the window.

Perhaps she ponders a lost childhood.

MADMAN'S HILL

The old stone barn has been pulled down now. Marion and Dan have used the stones for other building purposes. The old property at one time rang with the sounds of bushrangers invading the residence, and convicts who laboured for their masters.

The story still survives that one convict, maddened by the cruelties of the penal system, escaped and ended his life by hanging himself from a tree on the hill...hence the name: Madman's Hill.

Present owners of the property, as well as past occupants, tell of the difficulties in mustering sheep past the spot of death. The noise of a man screaming has been reported more than once. That sound has certainly unnerved many visitors.

About the middle of the 1980's, during a very dark night, the owners were working on the barn. The hanging tree still stood. Horses with which they were working went 'right off'. Dan let his horse's head go. It became frenzied and galloped home immediately. The sheep fled in chaos. But all of that can be explained. Of course it can. Or can it? The same story has been reported by others who took dogs, horses, or sheep by the old hanging tree. Not every time -- just sometimes -- the animals either freeze or go a bit crazy.

To prove to themselves that they had nothing to fear, Dan and Marion went back the next morning to the site of the episode of the night before. This time the horses refused to walk past the tree. The dogs stiffened and growled. The sheep stopped. Strange.

But the story of Madman's Hill does not end here. One day, Dan took Marion to an old cave which was now concealed by bushes. Signs of very old fires were in evidence. They recalled old Mrs. Chills who, at the time, was almost 100 years old. She said that it was common knowledge that Martin Cash and others had hidden out there at Ravensbourne and Gunners Point, close to Madman's Hill. It is believed that those escapees had hidden in that same cave as they tried to escape the horrors of the system.

Perhaps the very stones call out the dread of a time past, and that is why animals shy on Madman's Hill.

A POLTERGEIST

The same lady, Marion, seems to have a particularly sensitive spirit. Intelligent, handsome, and educated, she is not the sort of person who makes up stories. An evening with her will discover both wit and depth.

Marion is also a collector of stories of the past – not just strange tales, but stories of Tasmanian history.

Her family purchased a property not far from Madman's Hill. There they decided to build on a site different from the home that had been there in colonial times. Perhaps it is fortunate that they selected another place on which to build.

The old homestead was the sight of a tragic story. The daughter, falling in love with a bondsman (evidently a stone mason by trade), was forbidden to see him again. Such is tragedy enough: a Romeo and Juliet story. (It should be remembered that during colonial times, bondsmen were frequently viewed as the personal property of their masters.)

One day in June, the stone mason, who was no longer able to handle the separation, ran away. Evidently he was shot and killed during the escape...at precisely 4:00 p.m.

As Marion and Dan were building their new stone house (it happened to be a day in June at precisely 4:00 p.m.), a number of unusual things happened. Hammers and chisels disappeared. Dogs growled and bristled. These unusual happenings continued until July. The house also felt strangely chilly.

To this day, no one knows why the hammers and chisels turned up where the old foundation of the bygone house had been built. It remains a mystery.

The chill is gone today; nor do tools go missing. Perhaps the old stone mason is satisfied with the moving of the stone to the new locality. And the present residents are acceptable to his spirit.

ST. JOHN'S PARK

The old hospital of St. John's Park had been planned well before 1831, when it was finally finished. The early settlers of Hobart Town knew that a modern community needed the best sort of health care. The trouble is that the good intentions of people can sometimes be corrupted by carelessness or misuse.

So, while many good things took place at St. John's in the name of humanity, there were some venal acts as well.

The story is told of how some of the rich families of Van Diemen's Land began to use the hospital as a lunatic asylum and human dumping ground, as well as a hospital and orphanage.

Margaret, like Marion at Madman's Hill, shared an interest in strange and historical stories. An employee of St.Johns, she wanted to go on the rounds with a worker who told strange tales about unusual events which took place in the undercrofts and hidden cubicles of the hospital. They decided to go 'all the way': in other words, to make their rounds together in the full of the moon.

They said they heard a child's cry...pitiful and plaintive. "We walked to the base of some steps and saw a small and distinct glow ahead of us," Margaret said. They walked up two steps into the old building and the glow disappeared.

Taking their courage into their hands (or throat?), the two undismayed explorers continued their investigations. They had heard about the student nurse who had seen one of the patients in a night dress walking the corridors. She searched, but found nothing. It is said that the nurse heard a scream and, looking up, saw a woman disappear through a door into the old section.

She swore the door was shut.

All of this sounds particularly frightening, but there is another part of the story which will not disappear. It is said that some generations ago a tunnel was dug from the old hospital to a place just across from the Maypole Hotel. The tunnel has been the object of many searches, but has never been found. It could be that some of the cries in the middle of the night were those inmates who found the tunnel to the pub down the road! The cries could have been the shouts of hilarity.

But while the story of the pub tunnel is humorous, it does not account for the strange knocks heard by present professional staff and workers. Neither does it account for the story of the convict girl who was murdered and buried under the floorboards of the old church. It is said that a young girl is sometimes seen wandering outside of the old hospital, trying to enter.

But if that is the case, why doesn't she merely walk through the wall like a proper ghost?

But really, does it make any sense? The authors don't know. All that can be done is tell the stories as they are related.

We do know that in the old hospital, on the west wing, in the undercroft...are two cells. They were obviously used for convicts while the building was being constructed in the 1830's. Walk through the old building, and you can feel that many things have happened in Old St. John's Hospital, Hobart Town. If you are ever in the almost abandoned building – especially at night – perhaps you too will hear the knocking, knocking...at the chamber door.

The Grange
Dr. Valentine's window.

St. John's Park
Haunted staircase.

12

THE MURDERED STOCKMAN AND THE OLD KEMPTON INN

The old hotel is gone now, destroyed by fire and time. A splendid new hotel now stands in its place. The story of the stockman, however, continues to be told.

It seems that the eternal triangle of two men contending for the attention of a woman caused the problem. The stockman was stabbed and, not being fatally injured, made his way to the attacker's room.

Evidently, the serving lady was worried about one of the two men, one of whom was her boyfriend. She came upon them as fatal revenge was about to be taken.

Here the story goes a bit hazy, for knives were turned upon the lady as well as the stockman. Both died from their wounds. The second man escaped.

Through the years, there have been many strange tales about the serving woman and the stockman and how they wander old Green Ponds (now known as Kempton). However, it would seem that the destruction of the old Kempton Pub has quietened their spirits. They are no longer reported to be restless.

Or do the murdered spirits still look for their killer?

OLD ARTIE

One could say that the Bridge Hotel at Ouse died in the flood of 1929. From that time it festered for many decades, until someone saw its value and rescued the derelict building from death by mould and destruction. The new owners have an eye for value.

But Old Artie, who had previously been terrified at the hotel, was a man who liked a dare. He had a good sense of humour and liked adventures.

So, one night at a friend's house, stories of the strange and unexplained were being discussed (as they frequently are in Tasmanian homes). Artie dared Marcia to climb up the old steps to the second floor of the derelict Bridge Hotel.

Marcia accepted the dare.

Of course, it was a dark night. They had decided to wait until midnight for the full effect of their lark. Only part of the staircase was still useable. The rest had collapsed. Marcia clambered up the shaking steps to the top floor. She was quite pleased with herself. Leaning out of the window, she was about to tease Artie that he was a 'cowardly custard'. At that moment, Marcia (nineteen years old, a nondrinker, and strong from being in the saddle many hours a day) was suddenly touched strongly on the shoulder. It was a muscular and powerful hand which grabbed her. She flung her hand around to counter the clutching 'thing'. Nothing was there. No one stood behind her! She was alone. Her torch showed nothing.

Young Marcia screamed, of course, and ran down the steps. But there WERE no steps. In her terror, she had forgotten.

"Artie, it's him! It's him!" she shouted. The next thing she knew was that she had fallen down the hole in the steps, spraining her wrist and bruising herself. "Artie, we gotta go!" she yelled.

Artie was already in the ute and gunning the engine. They escaped. But from what?

Was the presence an old hobo who was sleeping there? But where was he? Why didn't her torch show anything?

But, happily, whatever it was which grabbed Marcia that night at the Bridge Hotel has gone to rest. It is no longer heard...or felt. Or so they say.

MAURISTON HOUSE AT THE HUNTING GROUND

Jacqueline and Alan Korobacz love their new home which they are carefully restoring to its colonial grandeur. Empty for many years, Mauriston will soon have the eminence it once enjoyed.

The Korobacz, both professionals in the legal field, are not the sort of people who make up stories. They also have a love of accurate historical reconstruction. As such, they have embarked upon a study of their property's history...as well as making a very comfortable home for their family.

As one drives from Dysart and views the grand old home from the road, one can only be reminded of the Georgian mansions of England. The sandstone gates and giant trees on either side of the lane bid an elegant welcome...as do the Koroboczs.

Mauriston House is the original home of Captain Clark. The Captain and the bushranger, Martin Cash, had met each other before Cash's holdup of the Clark homestead: when Captain Clark had dismissed charges against Cash and his wife Eliza. Martin, always an honourable man, recognized the Captain and is recorded as having said (in his book, MARTIN CASH), "...Captain Clark was the gentleman who (had) acted so generously." So Cash "...discontinued his business..." and left Mauriston House.

We do not claim Mauriston House to be haunted with the ghosts of Cash, nor of his bushranging partners, Kavanagh and Jones. There are, however, other strange tales about the old estate.

Poltergeists (ghosts which move things) seem to inhabit old Mauriston House. Jackie has had three single earrings go missing. They were dropped from the table and no amount of searching could discover their hiding place. They were found some time later at other localities far removed from the table. SOMETHING had moved them.

By itself, the poltergeist story means little...just a matter of forgetting things. However, what about the tourists who had an accident nearby? Almost as in a gothic mystery, the travellers were invited to stay overnight in the guest bedroom upstairs. During the night, a woman dressed in Old World clothing stood in the guest bedroom and watched the sleepers, Sensing her presence, one of the tourists awoke. The woman in old-fashioned clothing soon disappeared. Next morning, the reluctant guests queried the Korobaczs about the identity of the strange woman. (We can imagine what thoughts were going through their minds.)

Jackie told them quite clearly that she was the only other woman in the house that night.

And what about the upper class gentleman in the three cornered hat who appears in the garden from time to time – and who also disappears in a blink of the eye? A figure of a man also appears from time to time inside the house, usually standing by various beds. Perhaps it is the good Captain Clark. People who have seen the image feel no bad emanations. The man in the three cornered hat seems harmless enough.

Or...what about the young man who saw a lady lying on the chaise lounge when no one was in the house?

Or...things which go missing to reappear sometime later on the kitchen table?

Or...the soft music which can be heard from time to time and which has no observable origin.

Or...Alan's mother's experience with the earring which, seemingly, jumped off the card and disappeared.

Or...rings which go missing to turn up two years later -- ON A MOUND OF FRESHLY TURNED SOIL in the garden!

Jackie's mother also experienced a happening with her rings: they moved inexplicably. It would seem that the poltergeist of Mauriston House likes to play tricks. It would also seem that Jackie and Alan's 'presence' likes jewellery...and tricks. (Our guess is that the jewellery ghost is female.)

The Korobacz's have learned to live with these experiences with good grace and a sense of whimsy. It even makes living in the old mansion a bit of an experience. As they say, "No one ever gets hurt." And it certainly gives them things to talk about. They also know that Mauriston House was, for years, so feared by locals that no one would go near the old building. For Jackie and Alan that is fortunate. It is well known what happens to old vacant houses. The stories of the haunting probably saved the stately old home from vandals.

However, there is one somewhat chilling story that needs to be related more carefully. As they were being shown through the house, the authors were led to one of the front rooms. Buck was about to walk through a doorway when something forced him to stop: a 'presence' prevented his passage. He said the feeling was physical. He backed up, and Joan was about to make her passage through the same doorway. She too, felt a 'presence' in the same spot and stopped. One of the Korobacz's observed that other people also had trouble passing through the door. Maybe it is the spot where Martin Cash met Captain Clark. Something was certainly there!

But the real mystery of Mauriston House has to do with a doll – a doll with green eyes.

Miranda was not yet three years old when it first happened. She said that 'James' (a name she had given the doll) emerged at night from the eyes of her doll and 'did naughty things'. This happened a number of times. James' eyes continued to move, and James continued to do 'naughty things'. So, putting Miranda back in bed one night and noting that all was in order, Jackie returned downstairs. She came back later to look at the sleeping child (like any good mother). Besides, she thought she had heard a voice -- Miranda perhaps...or James.

Upon entering the room, Jackie crashed into the rocking horse...it had been moved from its previous place. Miranda was sleeping, but the rocking horse was moving back and forth as though someone had just dismounted...and it now faced the door. One of Jackie's scarves was tied neatly around its neck. Who did it? The child, who had quickly leapt into bed after carefully tying the scarf to the moving rocking horse? Hardly likely. Or...James?

One story does not make a ghostly tale. But, putting all the ghostly tales together, one has to admit to 'something' at Mauriston House.

But you should also experience the old barn behind the house. It was built around 1820 and was a barn and bunk house for the servants. It feels like few places feel in Old Van Diemen's Land...perhaps because it is one of the oldest standing buildings in Australia. There have to be a few ghosts here as well.

The Korobacz' have learned to enjoy their ghosts... and they will eventually have one of the finest old mansions in Tasmania. If the spirits let them.

We are sure they will.

Mauriston House. Magnificent, charming and fascinating.

And, dare we say...haunting?

Mauriston House
*At the Hunting Ground, the
green-eyed doll.*

Mauriston House
At the Hunting Ground.

KODAK HEADQUARTERS, HOBART

Her name is Beryl. She inhabits the fourth floor, but sometimes descends to the lower floors (including the basement) of the Kodak Building. It seems that Beryl is not just a friendly presence; it appears that she also likes to involve herself in a bit of mischief.

Ask the staff and of course they will tell you that poor old Beryl is blamed for anything which goes wrong in the old building. It must be nice to have a scapegoat at work.

Ask the police and they will tell you that they don't like to enter the premises if an alarm has been tripped. We have been told that the alarms which sound are frequently false.

Ask the Wormold Security people and they will tell a similar story: they don't like to enter the Kodak Building in the hours of early morning.

Sometimes the intercom activates and no one is on line. How can this be explained when there is no one in the building apart from a staff member working back at night?

One day a display of cameras fell; for no reason. The cameras had been securely stacked. So strong was the exhibit that one could sit on it with no danger of the display collapsing. Of course, they blamed poor old Beryl.

On the same day as the event of the event of the collapsing cameras, another strange thing occurred: the door on the fourth floor, always firmly fastened from the inside, popped open. A rush of wind blew in so hard that the door was difficult to secure. That same fourth floor is where footsteps are heard many times...pacing, pacing, pacing. The fourth floor is Beryl's special place.

If all these tales are not sufficient to make the hair on your neck become slightly elevated, there is the story of how a stack of files fell and were put back...only to fall down again shortly after. Of course, it must have been Beryl.

Caroline tells the story of how a young person is sometimes seen sitting on the steps to the second or third floor. Is she the ghost of a young woman who died in the building during the 1940s? Is the same entity responsible for chemicals being moved, lab lights being turned on and off, and for doors being inexplicably opened when they should be closed?

But, if the above experiences aren't enough to make one ponder about the 'other worldly' things, there is the story from Graeme. He had arrived in Hobart in 1988 and was taking up his new job with Kodak. Like any good, new employee, Graeme was working back one night. The radio was playing, and Graeme was concentrating on his computer screen. Thinking he heard footsteps on the stairs, he paused. When he returned to his work, the footsteps sounded again. Graeme got up from his desk and tiptoed to the door. Knowing about the ghost of Beryl, he was going to scare the person who was about to try to scare him. He jumped from the doorway, and...NO ONE WAS THERE!

Needless to say, Graeme went home rather quickly. Nor does he work late anymore...unless he has to, and then he makes sure a friend stays too.

And then there is the woman who was working late, and, on hearing the footsteps, hid under her desk! When the footsteps stopped, the lady beat a hasty retreat. Of course!

But we leave the story of Beryl and the Kodak Building with the tale related by Mr. Brown of Wormold. It seems that, along with the footsteps and the one special light socket which continually burns out globes, a young woman was seen by one of the security men...late at night. The lady wore a nightgown and had straggling hair. But she seemed friendly...for some reason...

When you buy your next supply of film from the Kodak Shop in Hobart's Mall, ask the staff if anyone has seen Beryl lately. They will certainly have a story or two to tell.

George Town
The Grove staircase.

Kodak House, Hobart
Beryl's basement.

ANIMAL GHOSTS

How about the ghosts of animals? Why NOT the ghosts of animals? If people have ghosts why NOT animals?

Andrew and Sheila both experienced the following three tales. Both people are professionals, educated and intelligent.

Their white manx cat, a loved family pet, had been run over by a car and had been buried in the back yard. During the night, Sheila heard scratching at the door...identical to the cat's scratching. She got up to investigate, wondering what in the world the noise was. While the scratching continued, she opened the door. There was nothing there

Andrew and Sheila also had a dog named Bo. Bo went to the happy kennel in the sky...or did he? He had been a friendly dog and the family shed a few tears as they buried him. On the following day, George, a friend of the family, came to visit. He was unaware of the death of the dog. When they told him of the death of old Bo, George was incredulous. "What are you talking about?" George asked, "When I drove up just now, Bo greeted me just like he always does."

If that animal ghost story is not enough, Sheila and Andrew tell another one: Pet rabbits sometimes catch myxo, and this had happened in the case of Andrew and Sheila's pet. Sheila had been comforting the animal, which was in a box on the kitchen table. She had just returned to join Andrew in the parlour when a grey shape moved across the floor. The grey shape had no special configuration: it was merely a 'grey shape'.

Andrew said something like, "Did you see that 'thing' move across the floor?"

Sheila nodded that she had seen the same grey shape. Thinking it rather strange, she got up to check the rabbit...only moments after she had last looked at it.

The rabbit was dead.

THE BICYCLE GHOST
OF ST. HELEN'S

Roy Towers of Goshen was a local identity. He was well known and liked by the locals. Roy, like so many bushies, neither liked nor trusted banks. He always kept his money with him.

So, when Roy set off on his bike for town, he carried what little money he had in a bag around his neck. After all, he was not in danger from local bushrangers knocking him on the head. However, he WAS in danger. You see, the bag, which dangled loosely, dangled a bit too far.

Old Roy was on his way to St. Helens along the dusty and bumpy Anson's Bay road when his money bag slipped...or he looked down at something while he was peddling. The bag became hooked up in the spokes of the bike, and old Roy fell, breaking his neck. He died very quickly.

It was a very unfortunate and unusual accident, and it was recorded in the press at the time. However, it is to residents and visitors of the area that the story becomes even more unusual.

People swear to this day that they have seen a 'person' or 'something' walking the road -- or apparently moving swiftly -- as if gliding. The apparition then disappears.

Perhaps Old Roy is still looking for the money which may have spilled from his bag.

Have you seen old Roy lately?

Norwich House, Norfolk Plains
The window.

The Bicycle Ghost of St. Helens
The path.

GOULDS COUNTRY...YOU CAN FEEL THE HAUNTING

One could call the tiny hamlet of Weldborough an almost nonexistent community, except for the pub and a few aged houses. Not many generations ago it teemed with people: miners, wood cutters, carters...the lot. Now, about all that can be said is that Weldborough is semi haunted. Semi haunted? You will have to go to Weldborough and Goulds Country to see what we mean.

Start with the cemetery at Moorina, close to Weldborough. The giant pine trees, which hedge one side of the drive, are sentinels to the dramas of the past. But the haunting really begins with the strange tombstone which was built many decades ago by the Chinese community which lived in the area. The cement chimney was part of an oven which offered food to the gods for the souls of the dead. The Chinese were miners, shop keepers, sly groggers...everything which European settlers were...with one exception: they tended to be more successful because of their willingness to work terribly long hours.

It was in cemeteries like Weldborough where Chinese bodies were exhumed. It is alleged that the families of dead Chinese miners buried treasures with the deceased in order to enjoy the joys of heaven more happily. Thus the grave robbers.

If the Chinese miner's grave managed to escape the plunderer, it was probably disturbed at a later date by the miner's family. The bones of most Chinese workers were exhumed and sent to final rest in the Middle Kingdom: the only place where a Chinese person could find ultimate peace.

Many Chinese ghost stories still circulate the north eastern corner of Tasmania.

The Star of Peace Mine at Weldborough has long since melded and moulded into the surroundings. There are only a few reminders: stones from an old fireplace, disrupted land, and scrub trees. Sometimes a light on top of Weldborough Hill is seen from Pyengana. The light disappears and reappears. No, it is not merely that of hunters spotlighting for roos and possums. People like Sandy Richards have checked on the lights many times. Sandy, a local bullocky and long time resident of the area, has seen the light three times and has enquired after its meaning. For some unknown reason, the light has long been attributed to a person of Chinese origins who was, perhaps, an early miner.

The story and the light persist in local lore. It is seen from the Pyengana Valley as you look up to the top of Weldborough...very close to the Star of Peace Mine.

Gould's Country
The haunting steps to nowhere.

The Swallowed Gold Sovereign
The Longford Bar, Racecourse Hotel.

The Lovely Lady of Richmond Gaol
The pinky-red lady was seen here.

Gould's Country
You can feel the haunting "Ghost Tree".

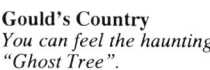

Norwich House, Norfolk Plains
Ruined out-houses.

Gould's Country
"Chinese Monument".

MYSTERY LADY OF PYENGANA

Sometime around the year 1970, the small farming community of Pyengana (near the Blue Tiers area close to St. Helens) experienced an odd happening. A mystery lady appeared in the area. She remained for a few weeks...and, then, just as quickly vanished. Who was she? Where did she come from? Where did she go? These are still questions asked by the locals who still live in the valley...for it is impossible to be anonymous in a Tasmanian hamlet.

Margaret Richards was probably the first person to see the lady. Margaret is Sandy's wife and they share an interest in and love of the community. The Richard's home, the oldest in the area, verges the bush and stands between the oldest and newest highways.

One day, Margaret was looking out the window, glancing up the old road as one will do in the normal course of daily life. She saw a lady dressed in old fashioned clothes. You know...the sort of clothing they wore last century.

"Odd," Margaret said to herself. Not knowing who this unnatural-looking, older person was, Margaret naturally wanted to keep an eye on the situation. Remember, the Richards' house is an old home with smaller and fewer windows than more modern homes.

Margaret went to the next window to see where the unusual lady was going. To do that she had to open a door, cross the center passage way and open the next door. In a matter of seconds, the old woman had disappeared. The mystery lady had vanished.

At that exact time, one of the Richards' children had arrived home from school. It would have been impossible for the daughter to have missed seeing the mystery lady.

"Where did that old lady go? The one who was walking in front of the house?" Margaret asked.

"What old lady, Mum? There was no one outside."

In Margaret's opinion, it would have been impossible for her daughter to have missed seeing the woman.

But the riddle does not stop there. The mystery lady appeared many times in the next two weeks; sometimes by old barns or old buildings.

Inevitably, when locals investigated, the old lady (still dressed in grandma clothes) had vanished without a trace.

This pattern continued for about two weeks before the Mystery Lady of Pyengana finally disappeared...but perhaps not for good.

Perhaps she was checking out her old community and found it quiet and pleasant. Like it is.

THE 'DOUBLE GHOST' OF PYENGANA

Why Pyengana, you might ask. We don't know. We DID tell you that the whole area around the Blue Tiers seems...well, exceptional. One could even say, as one explores the area and as one probes its history, that it does feel...HAUNTED.

There is the tale about 'the fellow who sits on the post in front of the tiny Anglican church'...right by the graveyard. The church and graveyard are on the narrow Tasman highway. The figure has been seen by at least two people who have told the story. They are people of good repute: solid farm people who aren't given to imagining things. They are no-nonsense folk. It is also rumoured that others in the community have seen the ghost.

Perhaps the 'ghost on the post' is explained by the following story: During the 1930's, a man (who we will call McSmith) decided that life was a bit too difficult for him. The Depression was full upon the farming community at the time...and life was very unrewarding. At the property which we will call Woods House, the man hanged himself.

Of course, he had to be buried and the family applied to the local priest for a burial plot. NOT POSSIBLE. The church would not accept his death as natural. He had committed suicide. McSmith would have to be buried OUTSIDE the graveyard and OUTSIDE the church property. What McSmith had done was very sinful in the eyes of the church of the day.

It just MIGHT be that the 'ghost on the post' is the same man who was not allowed admission to the church graveyard. His unmarked grave is on the other side of the fence.

Perhaps the ghost of McSmith is still waiting to get in!

Model Prison, Port Arthur
The fireplace.

The "Double Ghost" of Pyengana
The ghost on the post.

THE GOLCONDA GHOSTS

Like Weldborough, but even more so, the community of Golconda and the old Lone Star Mine has retreated into history. A hundred or so years ago, thousands of people searched for the tiny golden flecks...or served the miners in bars and stores. Today, barely a score of people live in the area. None of them make their living from mining.

The bush in the area – a mixture of semi rainforest and wet and dry schlerophyll – can be dangerous for the unwary bush walker. Local dogs have disappeared down abandoned mine shafts. It is a place that can be dangerous to both man and dog. Disrupted and disturbed many times, the land of the Panama Forest and environs must have resembled a moonscape a few generations ago. Now, happily, mother nature has almost forgiven those who dug and turned and cut the land. The hills have been partially restored by time and house the flora and fauna which makes Tasmania such a delight. (The same area around the Panama has also recently been the centre of an intensive investigation for the Tasmanian Tiger. The 'extinct' animal has been sighted by many people in the area.)

A few years ago a certain family said, "Enough of the city, the traffic, the crowds. We will live in the bush." So they purchased a piece of land at Golconda.

The family began to build a small home in the midst of the forest. But first they needed a temporary dwelling to camp in while they built their dream home.

An old miner's hut was nearby. "Better than a tent," Sally said. "Let's just have fun living in it while we build our house." The family moved in.

On the first or second night (Charlie can't remember which), a summer's full moon greeted the new residents.

"It was quite late," Charlie recalls, "and we had already fallen asleep. For some reason I woke up and peered up at the window... the one next to the old Dutch door. Someone was standing there. I could see by the light of the moon that the 'someone' was actually three people: a woman in heavy clothing holding a child, and a man wearing a great coat. The woman was smiling and gesturing with her bundle. There was no knock on the door," Charlie remembered. "They were just standing there...sort of smiling and beckoning.

"Sally," I said, "there's someone outside. They must have had car trouble and saw the campfire." We'd cooked outside that night, and the fire was still glowing.

"I got out of bed to see what they wanted. I didn't turn on the torch...it was so light...and went to the door. The three were still there, knowing, it seems, that I was coming. But how could they see into the room? I opened the door, and looked out to ask them if they needed help and...and...they were gone! Disappeared! Vanished.

"It occurred to me that someone was playing a trick, so I walked outside and looked around the hut. The trio was not there.

"Sally said I must have been dreaming, and I had to agree...sort of. Well, I must have been; after all, what else could it be? But a niggle continued in the back of my mind. I didn't really think I had been dreaming."

The family continued to work on their new home, building upon the foundations that had been laid years before. While digging, they found pieces of old bricks and evidence of fires. Most thoughts of the dream had been forgotten. Until one night.

It had been a perfect summer evening: friends, campfire, stories, wonderful weather, and the promise of another identical day ahead. The pressures of Sydney were far away.

Sally tells the next part of the 'ghostly' tale. "We went to bed fairly late. The campfire was still glowing enough to see the stumps which had been pulled around the fire. I was just settling down into bed and getting drowsy when I glanced out the window, hoping to see the little wallabies feed on the scraps we had left. Instead, what I saw were three figures sitting on the stumps which WE had just been sitting on. One figure was that of a woman in old clothing, and the other was (I think) a man. He was wearing a great coat. The third figure was small – a child I suppose.

"I didn't realize Charlie was awake too until he spoke. 'Sally,' he whispered, 'there are three people at the camp fire.' 'I wonder who they are?' Sally asked.

"'I don't know,' he said. 'I've been watching them myself. I'd better go and see.'

"Charlie got up, put on his robe, and went to the door. And when he opened it, the three figures...disappeared! Vanished! Gone!"

Time has passed for Charlie and Sally, and their children have all left home. The three figures have not been seen again.

Charlie says that if he believed in spirits he would say that the new construction had disturbed something. Perhaps the three figures had come to check on the newcomers. And perhaps they had found the new residents acceptable to their old surroundings.

How else can you explain it?

THE THREE SAILORS OF
FOUR MILE CREEK

Frequently referred to as 'the nicest beach in Tasmania' by more than the locals, Four Mile Creek is a kilometre of perfect sand and curling waves. It has its own diving rocks at one end of the beach, and a fresh water stream which affords safe bathing for small children. There are good left handed curlers for surfers just beyond the point . One would not go wrong to call Four Mile Creek an idyllic place.

But Four Mile Beach is also dangerous. It has an undertow and rocks a few hundred metres out. As recently as 1989 two people lost their lives in its waters.

One of the locals, an ardent fisherman who enjoys catching bream from the now-closed bridge, states that he does not like to be down there by himself in the dark. He says there seems to be a presence which makes his blood run cold.

Why, we might ask.

Perhaps the reason for the sudden chill goes back into time...perhaps to the Dreamtime. Not so long ago, the Aborigines camped on the shores of Four Mile...on the same headlands that we now enjoy. The testimony to Aboriginal presence can be discovered through the many middens in the area. It is not difficult, after a storm, to find traces of their passage through the district. Undoubtedly, if you are sensitive to such events, a quiet pause on the headland at Four Mile will recall some ghosts.

Recorded history does not say, but it is entirely probable that the sails of Captain Cook would have been seen from more than one of the Aboriginal kitchen middens.

The earliest recorded happenings took place soon after Hobart was founded and the whaling station at Falmouth was established. Approximately 150 years ago, an incident took place at Four Mile which may help contribute to the shudders of the bream fisherman on the now-closed bridge.

The story, as it has survived, tells of mountainous seas and of a ship foundering and sinking. In the midst of the tragedy, three men finally made it to shore. Exhausted, they crawled to safety. All other hands from the ship were lost.

Some time before the ship wreck, three men had escaped from the penal colony at Port Arthur (or one of its out-stations). The alert was given, and the word sent out. The communication would have been something like this: three convicts...east coast...escaped custody...dangerous...capture or shoot.

The scene returns to the rocky headland, just below the brow of the hill, on the south side of Four Mile Beach. Three sailors, almost drowned and thoroughly exhausted, huddled together for warmth. They were lucky to be alive.

The troopers arrived. Perhaps the sailors had been able to light a small fire, and perhaps that is what attracted the troopers. Anyway, the military men appeared over the rise...rifles drawn, cocked, and ready. The men they were hunting were desperados. And there they were! Perhaps the soldiers merely rode up and shot them. Perhaps the seamen jumped up and gave fight. In any case, the three forlorn sailors, mistaken as the escapees, were SHOT!

It appears that the soldiers quickly realized their mistake, and that there would be no reward for what they had just done. They consulted, swore each other to secrecy, and buried the three men where they had fallen. But stories like that cannot stay hidden. Eventually, the word leaked out about how three sailors had been gunned down. However, the soldiers retreated and undoubtedly escaped prosecution.

All was forgotten. But not quite. (Nor should it be.)

The legend still persists that sometimes...on still nights when there is a bit of moonlight...three distinct figures can be seen on the sands of Four Mile Creek Beach. They leave no footprints.

No one can ever prove such happenings, but perhaps you should walk the rock abutments and sandy shoreline one dark night...alone. Maybe (like the bream fisherman) you too will feel the tragedy of the three sailors who almost drowned...only to be killed by careless constables.

Perhaps you might even see them by the light of the rising moon.

Many Happenings at St. Andrews' Inn
Window where the sound of pebbles is heard.

The Three Sailors of Four Mile Creek
Beach where the sailors walk.

THE LIGHT IN THE BREWERY WINDOW

The story of the tragedy of the Large family at Swansea is one of Tasmania's well-known colonial tales...and perhaps the saddest. Let the diary of Grandma Travers tell some of it:

"April 9, 1918...I took the trip...to see the grave of my brothers and sister, six of them...drowned at the time of the wreck of the cutter 'Resolution' at Great Swanport on 5th November 1850. I was the first child born after the above happened on November 25th 1851. Got up at 1/2 past 7, had breakfast, then went to try and find someone to paint the stone...could not...saw the breakers coming in...saw a Hobart steamer coming along. It had to anchor till Saturday, a long way out, before it was able to come along side the jetty to unload because of the heavy sea..."

The cutter 'Resolution' was returning to Swanport from Hobart Town. On board was the Large family. The record shows that the weather was bad and getting worse. Like the Hobart steamer in Grandma Travers' diary, the 'Resolution' could not dock. By the time it had reached Waterloo Point, the sea was angry and the glass was falling. The captain, undoubtedly a man of questionable abilities, decided to keep the passengers on board while he and his men went ashore to drink at a local pub. One sailor was left on board to care for the ship and the Large family. A tragedy was waiting to happen!

The wind turned into a gale. The seas grew heavier and the small ship dragged anchor on the sandy bottom and was pulled a kilometre to the mouth of the Meredith River. The news travelled quickly: a ship and a family were in trouble!

A group of horrified and fascinated townspeople gathered. Frantic attempts were made to launch a boat. The waves were too high. But let Grandma Travers continue the story.

"...April 10th...I went to the Church of England rector, a Mr. Finten, to get permission to do the grave up. He was very kind and lent us a spade and offered to see to everything for me and to find a man to paint it and have the photograph of it taken...William cleaned the rubbish off the grave and dug it up. It was covered with cutting grass and gorse...He put the headstone up straight...I went to the beach which is close by and gathered some shells and put them on the grave in the form of an anchor...It looked very nice...April 11th...went to see a Mr. Shaw. We were told he might remember...He told us he was only 3 years old when it happened, but could remember his father talking about it. He said Swanport was a prison settlement in those days, and there was a Captain Lyons there at the time. He took a boat on a ? to the wreck and got 6 of the prisoners to go in the boat out to the wreck to rescue mother. She clung on to the rigging for 12 hours before they got her off. The boat only got a short distance out when it swamped with the breakers. The men then refused to go a second time. The Captain then went in the bush and got a big stick called a waddie and told the men to man the boat again and the first one that refused he would knock his brains out, so they made another start and reached the wreck and rescued mother. The six children were all drowned by that time. I don't know how father was saved but he was a splendid swimmer. They had been going to Swanport to open a brewery and they lost everything they had. Five of the childrens' bodies were washed on shore but one was never found. Mother and father were taken to a Mr. Meredith's till they recovered and then returned to Hobart. Returned to tea after spending a very sad day...April 13th...saw the spot where father was going to start a brewery. That part has all gone to decay...sat on the beach till dinner time...I showed (Mrs. Hunn) Mother and Father's photos and a locket with the children's hair...April 14th...He (Mr. Shaw) said that after Mother was brought to land a man was seen struggling in the water and he told a large strong prisoner that if he saved him he would get him a free pardon...so he plunged in and brought him ashore and got his pardon..."

Note: this diary was written by Clara Travers (nee Large), wife of William Thomas Travers. She was born in 1851 and died in 1943.

And the ghostly tale?

Schouten House, which was to house the Large family's prospective brewery, sometimes shows a mysterious light in an upper window. It has been seen and investigated many times. Each time someone enters the house to seek the source of the light, it disappears...and then reappears.

Perhaps the light is a lament – or memorial – for the six dead children of Elizabeth and Edmund Large.

And the grave is still there, leaning a bit, but tended better than it was in 1918. ...Many people over the generations have seen the light in Schouten House.

And, for some reason, it is always connected with the tragic story of the Large family.

The Light in the Brewery Window
Large childrens' grave Swansea.

Garth
Garth ruins.

GHOSTLY CORNER OF
THE BLUE TIERS

Alice Johnson is dead now. Unfortunately, it seems that no one recorded her stories. You see, Alice was a teller of tales...not tall ones, just Gould's Country tales. We were fortunate to have had tea with Alice many years ago, and we promised her that we would come back after our walkabout. Regrettably, she died before we were able to help her with her memoirs. Her friend, Mrs. Meech, still lives in an old home on the edge of Gould's Country. She too laments Alice's, passing and remembers her stories with good humour.

We were told about Ghostly Corner. As Mrs. Meech remembered, the story was about the house that was up the road a little from the tiny settlement. Children had played in the ramshackle place for many years, and they attributed strange things to the empty house. It was 'real spooky' they said. We remember Alice telling us that if we were 'real lucky' we might see a figure standing on the side of the road. People frequently did, she said.

We did as Alice suggested...perhaps it was because Alice was such a good story teller...and we were almost sure we saw 'something' at Ghostly Corner. Gould's Country, almost a cipher now, is like that...it FEELS weird. A 'presence' pervades the Blue Tiers, which is unlike that of any other place in Tasmania.

The old churchyard has an air of expectancy. And at the top of the mountain, fallen chimneys, old iron, and European trees tell of a community which has disappeared.

But if Ghostly Corner is not certified as haunted, there is the story from the old Lottah Mine that is sure to send a thrill. The story is about another light, similar to that of the light on Weldborough Hill. This light is on the road to the reopened mine at Lottah. Like the Chinaman's light of the Star of Peace Mine, this light has been investigated many times. It does not come from shooters. It is not from farm vehicles. The light comes and goes...a glow more than a light.

Drive down into the Lottah valley and perhaps you too will find a sort of 'power field'. Friends of ours did just that. They stopped at a place which seemed 'different'...strange. There, on a flat spot where a house had once stood, cement steps lead up to where a front door had once been. From where she was standing on those old front steps, one of the friends swore she saw a person hiding in what was left of the old garden. She went over to investigate...and there was no one there. To this day she swears she saw a person.

It seems strange that the glowing light of Lotta is seen in exactly the same place...at the foot of the steps which lead to 'nothing'.

That is weird enough, but recently, in Scottsdale, we met another lady who told us about a medium from Sydney who had stopped at her house. This medium said that the area of Gould's Country (which now houses an ashram retreat) was a very 'powerful point'...whatever that means. She just 'knew' it.

She felt a power not known to her before. This medium believes that at the precise location of the 'steps to nowhere', unique energy arrives from the very bowels of the earth.

We only report the story. Of course we don't believe it. Do you?

It all seems so improbable, and we fight hard in our minds not to succumb to the ghostly tales...especially to those around Gould's Country and the Blue Tiers.

BUSHWALKERS' GHOST

Why is it that so many stories about the Irish have to do with drink? When you visit Ireland, a warmer and kinder people you will not meet anywhere in the world. Nonetheless, Tasmanian ghost stories abound with Irish names...and Irish drinking and fighting and having a good time. This is another Irish story.

The man is merely known as the 'Wild Irishman'. We don't know his real name, but you might hear the Wild Irishman and his wife being talked about when you go on the Overland Track at Cradle Mountain.

The ghosts of the Wild Irishman and his wife are said to wander the mountains and tracks around Dove Lake. Legend has it that the Irishman was a gold miner and once worked a claim. 'Patrick', as we will call him, had two great jealousies: his gold claim and his beautiful wife. From his mine he would one day become very rich, and from his wife he could always bask in her beauty, knowing that other men wanted her as much as the gold.

The gold was difficult to find and his wife was difficult to keep. You see, if we follow the myth of the drinking Irish, she must have been Irish herself, because she kept grog in the camp and would get 'full as a boot' whenever she could. When the supplies ran out, so would she. When enough gold had been taken, the two would pack up, go to town, and have a good bash. And then they would return...you are right...penniless. Then they would continue digging and repeat the cycle.

As time wore on, the couple became well-known for their towering rages, fights, parties and making up. However, try as he might, Patrick could not keep his beautiful wife in camp. Frequently she would go off on her own and return penniless. Patrick was always willing to receive her back into his camp.

It is alleged by some that Pat decided to take care of things 'one day'.

That 'one day' came. Pat no longer worked his claim. People wondered where he and his beautiful wife had gone. No longer did they turn up at the local pub. They had simply disappeared.

45

To this day, it is said, a ghost prowls the camping environs of Dove Lake and Cradle Mountain. The ghost is supposed to be female, and, it is said, she appears to be lonely.

But don't let that worry you when you are on the Overland Track. The noise you hear is probably a devil or a possum...or just maybe it is Pat's wife...looking for a stashed bottle of grog.

THE MURDERED BARMAID OF SALAMANCA PLACE

The building is demolished now, and apparently the exorcisms of a visiting ghostbuster did the job of releasing the ghost of the barmaid of Salamanca Place, Hobart.

The building, constructed by convicts in the early colonial period, was used for many things, both legal and questionable, in the days of whaling. It is safe to say that Captain James Kelly would have been one of the frequent visitors to the old warehouse. Many unusual things happened there as well when part of the building was known as Ye Olde Cook House Tavern. The most memorable was the murder of the barmaid. It is said that she died a most cruel death... which, we suppose, would have probably meant rape and torture.

For years after her death, her hazy presence was sometimes seen moving in and about the warehouse, as if looking for something. Some were terrified by her presence. Others, like Foreman Drew of Ferguson's Hops, said there was nothing to fear as she was only a ghost.

It is just as well that the intrepid Mr. Drew had that attitude towards the ghost, for he worked late on many occasions. It was at those times that he heard breathing close by as well as sighs and murmurs. Mr. Drew said that it was as if the presence was about to ask him a question. Frequently, he said, the sightings and feelings took place at midnight or thereabouts.

Those sounds and sighs and sightings of the murdered girl gave ample reason for many of the workers to refuse to work overtime. One cannot help but wonder if the story was an old ploy by which management kept costs down!

But when Dr. McBain from Scotland was visiting Hobart, he heard about the ghost and the murder at Ye Olde Cook House Tavern. He decided to do something about it, and, being a celebrated exorcist, released the poor dead girl's soul...or so the legend goes.

Really, it seems a shame in a sense, for what replaced the old warehouse? Right...another warehouse. Perhaps it is more modern and profitable...but the ghost of the barmaid is gone, and with it another part of Old Van Diemen's Land.

We venture to say that there would have been more tourist dollars in the enterprise of a resident ghost in an old convict warehouse than in a modern building with air conditioning.

THE BARE BONES OF FRED AT THE ROYAL

There are so many stories about Fred, the ghost of the Theatre Royal in Hobart, that it seems we should try to get to the heart, or bone, of the matter.

Fred is supposedly the protector of the theatre, and is supposedly seen during performances, practices, or late at night. He is not malevolent, they say, only protective.

It would seem that Fred wasn't always passive, for evidently he was one hard and heavy drinker in the days when the Theatre Royal was also a tough pub.

It is said that Fred was an actor whose professional qualifications were considered poor. Never mind that: Fred was supposed to be good with a bottle. As a boozer of heroic proportions, Fred used to rage with his mates in the pub in the lower basement of the theatre. The pub, known as Shades Tavern, is a poorly disguised attempt at saying 'Hades', for that is what it was...Hell. As well as a watering hole for theatre personnel and patrons, Shades Tavern was also a tough waterfront bar with nefarious port-siders as frequent customers.

It was during the early 1840's (or thereabouts) that Fred met his match and was killed in a brawl. We imagine that he was probably buried at St. David's and that a good time was had by all at the wake which followed. In fact, it is a nice thought that the wake may have been so good that Fred decided to never leave the Theatre Royal.

Shades Tavern continued its shady ways: prostitutes sold their wares and used the private boxes in the theatre or dark spots in the undercroft, and crowds of drinkers took part in many more brawls. It is said that performers had to sometimes fight their way to the make-up rooms in order to get ready for the night's performance.

But through it all, there was Fred...sometimes cloaked, sometimes in costume, but usually a friendly apparition...intent on protecting his territory. He was seen, and still is, flitting along the passage ways, always inquisitive.

When a recent fire almost destroyed Australia's oldest theatre, it is said Fred came to the rescue. The conflagration started near the stage

49

and the curtains quickly caught the flames. There was no other thing for the burning curtains to do than to fall onto the stage. If that had happened, everything would have been destroyed in an inevitable inferno. But no! Somehow our intrepid Fred managed to cause curtain to fall into the front rows of the theatre. Alarms sounded, firemen arrived in time, and Fred's theatre was saved.

Today, the Theatre Royal is better than ever after being wonderfully restored from the smoke. And now a fire screen separates the stage from the auditorium...

And Fred – if we can isolate fact from fiction – is still there, flitting, ephemeral and wraith-like, protecting what he sees as his.

And Shades Tavern? It will take much money to bring the old watering hole back from the perdition of the past; but when one day it is completed, you can be sure that Fred will be down there, too.

We think that he might be waiting for another wake.

The Commandant's House,
Port Arthur
The Rocking Chair.

The Bare Bones of Fred
Fred's chair at
Theatre Royal, Hobart.

BLOOD AT BONA VISTA

It might be said that blood on old sandstone steps hardly constitutes a ghost story, but there is something about the old home of Bona Vista which makes for a shuddering tale. We think we know why.

In 1853, the bushrangers James Kelly and Andrew Dalton were known to be at large in northern of Tasmania. They were desperate and willing to kill. This they did at Bona Vista...not far from Avoca and the legendary Garth. Who would have thought that the three metre high stone fence could have been so easily overcome? The fence had been built to hold out the most desperate bushrangers and the wildest Aborigines. But times were more relaxed in the 1850's than they had been thirty years before when Matthew Brady strode the land.

Tasmania was just beginning to throw off the evil reputation it had received as the penal colony of Van Diemen's Land. Transportation was about to end. A new day dawned for the small colony. Bushranging was also coming to an end.

In the classic mode of Cash, Kavanagh and Jones, Kelly and Dalton 'bailed up' the inhabitants. This meant that they boldly strode onto the property with their fingers 'on their triggers', hammers pulled back, and defiance in their eyes. It almost always worked. Who would not back down?

Immediately, servants and workers were tied up securely. Having some proper consciousness of class, the bushrangers tied up the owners and made them sit in the dining room. Then, while one of the outlaws kept an eye on the prisoners, the other ransacked the home. After a good long search, many things of value were placed in bundles.

It is thought that Kelly and Dalton stayed overnight, no doubt enjoying the fruits of their labour. Needless to say, they began to drink. We assume that most of the household were either kept locked in their rooms or were tied up.

We can assume that by morning the bushrangers must have been fairly drunk. We can also assume that the workers who were supposed to have reported for work on a neighbouring property were missed. Four policemen were sent to investigate...with one gun! A shoot-out took place, and one constable fell, apparently dead. It was then when

Constable Buckmaster made his dash. Through the front door he leapt. Dalton, a good shot, aimed and fired. Buckmaster caught the charge in the head. He fell on the steps. There he died and there his blood sank deeply into the sandstone.

For decades, Constable Buckmaster's blood could not be cleansed from the steps. Wednesday was the day to clean the verandah. Try as the servants might and scrub as they would, the blood would reappear again. Nothing would remove the stains. And so the story of Buckmaster's ghost persisted.

Not much of a ghost story? No, we suppose not. But tie this together with the underground cells where the scores of convicts were kept at night, and the tale deepens. What degradations took place beneath the ballroom floor?

It was said that there was another ghost...a convict's presence...which used to wander Bona Vista. He was bloody and raw-backed, perhaps from the cat-o-nine tails. The convict was seen by many people over several generations.

Not many people are willing to spend a night at Bona Vista. We don't know why exactly. Perhaps it is the powerful feeling of impending doom. It is the same feeling of doom which probably explains why the old home has been abandoned for so many years.

And Dalton and Kelly? They made their way to the mainland and were finally caught in Melbourne. They were tried and hanged.

Perhaps they too have come back to wander the old ruins of Bona Vista...and to survey the blood.

LEG IRONS
AT WESLEY DALE

The EXAMINER EXPRESS of May 5, 1978, says it as well as can be said, '...Periodically, usually on stormy nights, about midnight, you will hear the sound of dull, heavy measured tread on the little staircase from the kitchen...the clanking of leg irons...the long drawn tinkling sound of chains being drawn through fingers...as nearer to the bed come the sound of steps...'

Wesley Dale, near Mole Creek, is one of the oldest farms in the north of Tasmania. The property is not a show piece like Clarendale because it is still a working farm. So has it been since 1835 when the Methodist lay preacher, Henry Reed, had the first buildings constructed. It is the same Henry Reed who was involved in the building of Macquarie House in Civic Square, Launceston, and who was involved in most aspects of life and politics in old Van Diemen's Land. He was a man who did his duty as he saw fit. Word has it that he was a strict but fair man. It has also been said that he was very quick with deals which would give him land or wealth. Henry Reed is also known for having been involved in the building of a number of chapels...and making his servants go to church...no matter what.

At Wesley Dale, walls over three metres high were built to keep out the Aborigines and bushrangers, and one can imagine that the very strict Methodist parson would not have hesitated to clap someone in irons for breaking the rules of the house.

It is not known why the ghost of Wesley Dale has not been seen for many years. It could well be that, whatever the presence was, it must be well satisfied with the present owners...or is it true what we hear on the Tasmanian bush telegraph? It has been rumoured that the ghost of Wesley Dale is still alive and making noises...thumpings, clankings, and the sound of footsteps close to beds.

We hope so.

GARTH

So much has been said about the 'Ghost of Garth' that the story is an enigma wrapped in legend. It has been difficult to separate the various layers. We will divide it into three parts: history, legend, and story. You can then take your choice of which is real and which is not.

The history of Garth is that Charles Peters was born near the South Esk River in Scotland in 1797 where he later leased a small bit of land on a farm called Garth. The Enclosure Laws were making it very difficult for small landholders to make a living. So, young and filled with fire, young Charles had come to Tasmania as a ship's crew member in 1823. He applied for land and it was granted to him in 1826. Like most young men of the time, he sought a wife. He found her and he and Susan Wilson were married at St. John's, Launceston.

Obviously, he had few funds and took a job at Malahide, Fingal, as a supervisor. Then, in 1830, he was granted 320 acres near Fingal. He called it...Garth. We guess that he was a bit homesick.

Their two year old daughter, Ann, died in 1840 after her clothes caught on fire. She was treated as they were in those days: lime water and oil! Ann's body was buried a few hundred yards east of the homestead. The grave and stone have recently been restored by the Marshall family.

By 1843, when Garth was fairly well completed, eight male employees and six children called the grand old property 'home'. How many women worked there is not recorded!

The house was passed on to members of the family, and in 1851 the stone house was badly damaged by fire. A few years later, another part of the house was destroyed by fire. By 1880, much of Garth was in disrepair...and other families moved in and out. Finally, in 1959, what remained of the shell was burned to the ground.

So much for the lineal history.

The legend about Garth is that the land was originally granted to an unknown Englishman early in the Nineteenth Century. He arrived, ready to build the perfect mansion for his bride-to-be who he had left behind in England. Together they would build a perfect property, have perfect children, and build a perfect piece of England in Van Diemen's Land. He began to build with imagination and strength. Convicts would have been assigned to him. Servants would have waited upon him. He was a gentleman.

Garth was to be a large house with large rooms, servants quarters, kitchens, serving rooms, dining rooms...It was also to be an English gentleman's home with English trees and gardens and a long stately entrance. House well under way, the unknown English gentleman went back to England to collect his bride. On arriving, he found that she had not been very patient...she had married someone else! Crushed, the man returned to Van Diemen's Land and there, in the courtyard of the home, he committed suicide. It is said that his ghost still roams the ruins and moans for his lost love.

The legend has a wonderfully mournful tone to it. However, the story, as it has been unravelled to a greater or lesser degree, is that the mystery also surrounds the death of a young girl at Garth.

The girl was high-spirited and tried the patience of her convict nanny. It would seem that the nanny was not the best of sorts. (We wouldn't have let her raise our child!) Nanny's threat was that if the young girl did not behave herself, she would take her and throw her down the well. It must have made a lasting impression on the young child!

One day, it is said, the girl did something particularly nasty and became afraid of what the nanny would do...so, in her terror, the young girl jumped into the well and drowned. The nanny tried to save her charge but fell into the well (as well!). She,too, was drowned.

The story goes that their cries can still be heard on dark nights...although today the well is pretty well filled.

Further research shows that an elderly member of the Peter's family remembers that the family in question had a young Asian (Aboriginal?) girl who lived with them. A pet lamb butted her into the well and she drowned. This latter girl is buried in Avoca and may well be the source of the cries.

Now, which do you choose; legend, story, or history?

It doesn't matter, we suppose, but if you stay at the tourist accommodation of Faulty Towers (owned by the Marshalls who are also the present owners of Garth), you will have the chance of walking over to Garth and inspecting the ruins. It IS chilling, and some people swear they can hear a child crying. Others attest to the truth that the presence of a man can be seen wandering the ruins of the courtyard.

Whatever the truth may be, Garth is a memorable destination for those interested in strange happenings and strange tales.

Garth
Garth ruins.

The Bare Bones of Fred
Chandelier of Theatre Royal.

Garth
The young girl's grave.

Norwich House, Norfolk Plains
The haunted hallway.

THEY CALL HER GUINEVERE

This is a difficult story because it doesn't make any sense. Some ghostly tales have a nice compact way about them: death by violence a long time ago followed by noises, apparitions, witnesses, and, finally (sometimes), an exorcism which makes for a happy ending. Some ghostly tales are merely inexplicable. This is one of them.

This is the story of a very solid Tasmanian family who have owned businesses, traveled the world, and raised responsible children to do responsible things. They are about the last people you would expect to have a household spook...but they seem to have one. They call her Guinevere and don't know why.

The haunting began some years ago when they bought a 100 year-old home in Launceston.

About twenty years ago, the authors were in the home of the solid Tasmanian family, and...as talk will turn to various things...they gave the following account of their old house.

"We had experienced many strange happenings in the house, but dismissed the sounds and incidents as merely being the workings of an old building. For instance, the doors were frequently opened when we knew they had just been shut. At first we blamed the children. Who wouldn't? Then we began to realize that it wasn't they who had left the doors open ALL of the time.

"One night, Johnnie and I went to bed. We were no sooner settling down to sleep when we sat bolt upright as the door shut on its own...and we saw the handle move before our very eyes. Needless to say, we were bothered. When you raise children you don't need any more problems.

"Anyway, our ghost seemed to be a young woman who had been a nursemaid or servant and occupied a tiny room at the top of the stairs which overlooked the garden. We could frequently hear footsteps of a smallish person, with the stairs creaking and doors softly opening. Whenever we checked, there was nothing...nobody...only open doors.

"While we lived in the John Street home, our middle child began to get very bad feelings from the house. In fact, it was one of the reasons that we decided to move. He would NEVER go upstairs on

58

his own and would fall asleep on the landing. He told us that the house was bad for him. We came to believe it.

"Once we had some Jewish friends come to stay with us. They believed differently from us, and spirits were part of their beliefs and understanding. The husband told us that he was aware there was a 'something' in the house.

"So, with our family, we moved to another home in Launceston, and for a number of years there were no noises and no sounds. It was very nice.

"The children grew up and left home, so we moved again; this time to a home in West Launceston which had been built in 1929. As you know, it is a very comfortable and gracious home. After we had been in the house for about four or five years, we began to hear noises...the sort of noises we had heard at John Street. Doors opened and shut...sounds persisted. My husband, Johnnie, saw the presence of a woman a few times. He would shake his head and let the image 'go'.

"A number of times I thought that Johnnie had come home early from work...when I heard the front door open and shut again. Just like before. More than once I called out, 'Johnnie, is that you?' I would go into the hallway and there would be no one there. I was alone in the house. I know that. It made me wonder if I was going crazy as I continued to hear sharp sounds, doors open and close. But Johnnie has continued to see the image of a lady. I guess we have learned, once more, to live with the spook.

"And, oh yes, a priest was called into the house on John Street by the later occupants. They wanted him to exorcise the place. He told them it was a friendly spirit."

Authors' note: Is it possible (IF there are such things as spirits) that, if the presence of the friendly lady was exorcised from the first house, it took up residence with some old 'friends' who already knew her ways?

There are strange things done under the midnight lights!

THE SWALLOWED GOLD SOVEREIGN

The Racecourse Inn at Longford was built in the early 1800's and was a friendly pub along the road to Cressy and Launceston. Although the bar is quite small, it is very easy to imagine how the traveler could easily have sat on a stool or chair to share the time of day with mates. We guess that the Racecourse Inn was a working man's pub.

One day, two workers from Cressy Farm (a few miles down the road toward Cressy) stopped off at the pub. They were feeling very good that day. One of them had a gold sovereign. We can see him slapping his money down on the bar and telling the barmaid proudly, "Two large rums, if you please."

The barmaid had learned a trick or two in her days. She picked up the small gold coin and...swallowed it! She was caught in the act and...well...you can imagine that the workers did not take too kindly to the act.

One of the men was overheard to say that they would deal with her later. They did. Later that night the barmaid was caught, killed and...need we be graphic? Let's just say that the two workers got their money back.

But the two men were also caught and were later tried for murder in Launceston. They were hanged on Gibbet Hill near Perth.

And the haunting? The present owners of the Racecourse Inn are not aware of any noises or bumps in the night. But, ask almost anyone who has lived in the community and they will tell you tales which make your hair straight.

One local Longford business man tells about how, as a kid, he and his brother stayed in the attic over night. He said they heard so many moans and noises and sounds that they fled while it was still dark. They spent the rest of the night outside in a field.

But why do we let spirits (if there are such things) worry us? They do no harm. Perhaps.

The Swallowed Gold Sovereign
Door to the bar, Racecourse Hotel.

The Hallway
*The staircase at The Grange,
Campbell Town.*

MANY HAPPENINGS AT
ST. ANDREW'S INN

It was around 1972 when the Rankin-Reid family decided to restore the old Georgian building in Cleveland, on the Hobart-Launceston Highway. It was an exertion of affection, for the old coach house had almost fallen down. It was worth it, for if the Rankin-Reids had not renewed the structure, Tasmania might have lost one of its better 'haunted' venues.

The Rankin-Reids noticed very quickly that 'things' took place in their new home. Objects moved and sounds were heard.

It was not only the Rankin-Reids who experienced happenings. The subsequent owner – before Joan and John Green took over – saw a strange-looking woman who entered her daughter's bedroom. Later, their seven year old asked, "Mummy, who was that lady who kissed me?"

When the Greens were looking for a new life style, they stopped for lunch at St. Andrew's. They arrived a bit early to get a good look, we suppose. They say that as they entered the old inn they felt that someone had physically 'cuddled' them. "It was warm and fuzzy," John said. "Very difficult to describe."

And so, the Greens took over. They hired an apprentice chef who was to sleep in the room above the bar. He unpacked his gear...and the next morning his work boots had been moved to the other side of the room. Alright, maybe he forgot.

Joan and John have both heard music...singing, opera...faint and fuzzy. They have no neighbours, so it had to come from the house. But no one else was home.

On the way to use the bathroom one night, John felt as if he had run into a brick wall. He could go no further. It seemed impossible to continue.

One evening, while sitting in the bar while doing the till (John says that everyone else was in the restaurant at the time), John heard footsteps in the room above...walking back and forth, back and forth. There was no one upstairs! It was on the same day that Joan and the chef, who were the only ones in the Inn, heard footsteps. Joan thought that John was back from the airport early and went upstairs to greet him. No one was there!

Add to that the time a friend thanked Joan for folding his clothes and putting them on the bed. They had been in his luggage on the floor. Joan informed the friend that she had not touched the clothing. No one else was home!

There are more things to talk about at St. Andrew's Inn...such as the small pebbles which bounce off the window of the back bedroom. It is said that Eliza Cash spent an evening there. And there are more tales and unnatural occurrences. The best way to find out the latest tale is to stop at the old coaching inn and ask Joan or John. They have a good, healthy attitude towards their resident ghost(s)!

NORWICH HOUSE, NORFOLK PLAINS

The above name is a nom de plume for a wonderful old colonial house. It is not a 'great house' in the sense of some other antique homes. Instead, the word 'venerable' comes to mind. Valiant attempts are being made to restore Norwich House, and if those attempts are successful, one of the more important rehabilitations in Tasmania's recent history will have taken place.

The home was built by Gov. Arthur's son who was, at the time, police commissioner of Norfolk Plains. (It is difficult not to think of 'jobs for the boys'.) Evidently, Norwich House was THE place in the community. Not just convict and police happenings took place there, but parties and public events were common.

A recent flood of the South Esk River seemed to have given the final death blow to the old home. Into this unhappy jumble, a family arrived. The Dorn's (not their real name) saw the line of trees, the quiet river, the pastoral warmth of the environment, and rightly fell in love with the home. They would fix it. The Dorns are the kind of people who can do just what they said they would do...and they are doing it.

But this is supposed to be a ghostly tale of Tasmania. Why the preamble? We give this introduction because the Dorn's are a very unique family. It is almost as if they are people who attract the spirits...but then, we forgot...we are not supposed to believe such things. We are merely collecting stories. IF there are spirits, then the Dorns are people who have a special sensitivity towards the emanations.

When the family arrived in the home, which was still dank from the flood of a few years before, Marilyn smelled jasmine in an unused part of the house. It was the part of the house that she felt was most strange. She was not acquainted with jasmine particularly, but she somehow 'knew' what the smell was. Something told her. Previously, she had been fearful of walking into that part of the house. But the odor of jasmine seemed to make things better.

Upon investigation, it was discovered that right where the odor of jasmine was most fragrant, a previous owner of long ago had cultivated some jasmine vines. The old lady loved jasmine and grew it abundantly. However, the jasmine plants had long since gone. Only overgrown weeds remained... and the smell of musk from the damp wood...and the odour of an old house. But Marilyn smelled jasmine. She knows what the smell is now.

A previous tenant had become terrified in the course of living in the homestead...because of the doors which kept banging and shutting, as if with anger. Some years later, it was found that the same tenant had been taking brass fittings and selling them. From what oral tradition suggests, it appears that the doors quit banging angrily when those tenants moved away!

The Dorn's children, having the same sort of sensitivities as their parents, have also felt the presence. Only once or twice has the presence been negative...but it merely depends on what you see as being negative. The children have reported how their doonas felt as though there was pressure being exerted. "Just like another blanket or something was being placed over me..." one of the children said. Needless to say, the young girl was frightened and went to sleep with mum and dad. This has happened more than once. Son Tom has heard mysterious foot steps and tapping sounds. So has his mother.

Karen has the only scary tale to tell. She always did feel uncomfortable in the large sunny room which had become her bedroom. Like her siblings, she too had often felt the pressure on her doona as she fell asleep. Sometimes she could see the doona moving...as if a cat was walking on the bed.

One evening, Karen was sure she saw the shadow of a hand in the window. Of course she became frightened. She woke her mum and dad, and thereafter slept with a rosary...which helped.

One night, while falling asleep...here is the scary part...Karen felt something running up her leg. "It was like a ball," she said. The next morning she had bruises on her thighs. The bruises were the same size as fingerprints.

One would think that by now the Dorn family would have gone to another property. They are not like that. No one pushes them around...not even ghosts.

So the family life continued. Marilyn got another crucifix and moved her daughter's bedroom and put in a pool table where the bed had been. That's the sign of a strong will.

Norwich House, Norfolk Plains
The skylight.

Old Falmouth Post Office
If it's not haunted, it should be.

But it was in the back section of the house where 'things happened' most. Interestingly, the hot spot for visitants in the house is close to the old prayer room or chapel. It is there where sounds of people can be heard – murmuring and talking. Marilyn thought it might be a radio outside. She checked it out. Nothing.

But even a tough minded person like Marilyn can get unnerved. But, to be accurate, it was really Lady the dog who gave the alarm. Lady, a friendly animal, was not happy with what was outside. "She became a wimp," Marilyn said. "She just went into the other room and cringed. For no reason. It happened twice. Now, that DOES scare me."

What about Gerry, Marilyn's husband? What does he do and see...and hear? To begin with, he is busily restoring the old home. He has a love for the old place and feels warmly akin to the spirits, if they exist. He proudly shows some of the freshly painted and decorated children's rooms. He is not about to let a few spirits get to him. (We remind the reader that about one half of the ghostly tales we have been told seem to have something to do with building, renovation, tearing down old walls, or ripping out old doorways.)

Perhaps the Dorns will get tired of the games ghosts seem to play, and perhaps they will move. But if they do move, we don't think it will because the ghosts got to them. It will be because they wanted to move...perhaps to train some more spirits.

THE LIGHT IN THE MIRROR

This is the story of Mary and Glen. They are average, hard working people who know life's up and downs. They love their family and don't kick dogs or wring the necks of birds...the sort of people with whom it would be fun to have a night on the town.

Mary had been ill and in the hospital and Glen was hoping to have some wardrobes built by the time she returned. (Note: there is the building theme again.)

One night after the hospitalization, Mary was awakened by something and looked into the new mirror on the wardrobes. A row of crosses were glowing there. The crosses were reflected into all the mirrors. 'Dreaming' was, of course, what passed through Mary's head.

Next night she was awakened by the same lights in the mirrors, and this time she looked into them to see that her face was distorted and twisted...screwed up as if it was made of plasticine. It was even painful...and there was the cross in the mirror again. Sounds like someone on LSD? Not Mary!

The third night came. Mary was almost afraid to go to bed.

Of course she was fearful, for that evening there was a presence in the mirror. It told Mary to KILL...to do damage. She had to fight off the feeling. There was no cross that night. This message continued for two or three more nights. A classic case of paranoia? No, not Mary...she had a family to care for. She overcame the power that came from the mirror – the awful power which told her to do evil.

Mary says that it was personal strength which saved her; and her strength was based on her faith.

The experience, Mary says, was real. "I wasn't sleeping.

I know that!"

Mirror, mirror on the wall...?

THE GHOSTLY SMELL OF BRICKENDON

It is with a considerable sense of humour that the Archers of Brickendon, Longford, speak of their 'ghostly smell'. The reader will note that ghostly smells are not unusual in Tasmania: flowers, musk...and Brickendon's smell are but a few.

The Archer family has lived on the same property for six generations and show every sign of being in the same home for six generations to come. That being the case, they have become used to their very special presence.

The odour, which seems to have no source, invades from time to time...sometimes at dinner parties, to the amusement (and mild embarrassment) of guest and patrone.

In times past, we can imagine people at the dinner table acting as if all was normal as the insidious odor spread its corruption through the assembly! Then, finally, from the head of the table, the presence of the 'eau de cologne' would have been suggested. We, too, share the humourous pictures created.

The result of the odour's presence has sent successive generations of Archers through the grand old home seeking the source. From cellar to attic, investigations have been conducted for the origin of the 'ghost'. He or she has never been discovered...if a smell has a gender.

The odour is no respecter of time, people, or place. The scent just makes its presence known.

What does a 'ghostly odour' smell like? "Sort of like rotting fish," one of the Archers bemusedly said.

The stink comes and goes, and there has been no way of predicting its impending arrival.

So, being warned is being forearmed, and now guests are told about the ghostly odour of Brickendon...and everyone has a laugh about the whole affair.

We cannot help but think that the Brickendon ghost has a definite sense of humour. So do the Archers.

GHOSTLY BIKIES!

It was a pea soup Tamar fog. The kind of fog when no one goes out. The kind of fog when one cannot even see the end of the car's bonnet. The kind of fog which causes all sounds to be muffled. The kind of fog in which no one should be about.

The kind of fog which FEELS evil!

Dave and Gary were good mates and still are. Each Saturday evening they would get together with each other's family at one or the other's homes. They would have a few beers, play some cards, talk, and generally enjoy a low-key evening out.

As they never kept libations in their home, the pattern had developed that Dave and Gary would drive to the Exeter pub, play a few games of pool, buy a few beers, and return home to the party. There the evening would pass pleasantly as it had so many times before.

Even though the fog was thicker than they had ever experienced, Gary and Dave decided that they had to follow through with the usual procedure. It was part of their mateship.

It was a very slow drive to the pub...the fog being so dense. Both windows were rolled down so they could see the road, and more than once they thought they had made a wrong decision to be out on such a night. But they finally arrived at the pub. There were no other cars in the parking lot. Good, Gary and Dave would have the pool table to themselves.

But there were two wonderful bikes out front. Two Nortons. Dave and Gary remembered how one day they had both agreed that Nortons were their dream. When their 'ships came home', they would have one each. They paused, touched, fingered, and stroked the machines. Both had been kept in perfect working order. One day, they both thought. One day!

Inside the pub, there were no sounds except from the two bikies who were playing eight ball. Even the balls seemed quiet.

Dave and Gary ordered a beer each, as well as a few bottles for the night's party. Then they waited for their weekly tickle with the cue. And they waited.

Finally, one of the bikies (who was dressed in perfect leather, studs, and boots which could only come from a place like Melbourne...Rossie boots they were) asked, "Wanna game?"

"Yeah, why not?"

So they played. At one point in the first game, Gary was lining up a shot for the corner pocket, normally a very easy pot. He looked up at one of the bikies who happened to be staring down the cue and ball..a normal procedure.

"Oh, my gawd.." Gary said to himself. The bikie looked strange. Gary shook his head and looked again. The bikie had teeth. Strange teeth. Fangs! Fangs like in a werewolf movie. Gary fumbled his shot and went over to Dave.

"Damn...did you see what I saw?" he asked.

"Yeah, I think so. Did YOU see what I saw? The teeth...the..."

"Let's get out of here!"

"Too right!"

"Where ya going?" one of the bikies asked, his teeth now retracted.

"Home. Gotta get back to the missus," was Gary's quick reply.

"Where do ya live? Maybe we'll drop by."

"Ah, never mind. Gotta go. Bye for now."

Gary and Dave split very quickly. On the way home, they imagined they could see lights following them. Lights which never gained or passed. Over and over they compared notes. They had both seen the same things.

At home, the two brave billiard players retold their story and drew pictures of what they saw. Now everyone was fearful!

So...two blokes had learned to scare locals in order to win at pool. Big deal. In fact, a good idea. Might try it ourselves.

Not quite. The vision of the two bikies, and their motorcycles would not leave the minds of Gary and Dave. In the morning they would solve the problem. They'd go see Charlie the barman who was also a good friend.

Next morning, being a Sunday, Gary and Dave drove over to the Exeter pub. It was clear and cool. The sort of day which almost always follows a fog.

71

"Charlie," one of the men said, "you know those two guys...the bikies in leather who were here last night? The ones who were playing pool...?"

"What bikies?" Charlie asked.

"The two guys we played pool with last night. The ones in leather. You know."

"What are you talking about? The place was empty. You two were the only customers we had all night. No one would go out on a night like last night...only you two."

"Come on..."

"Come on? You guys came in, played pool, talked a lot, and left real quick."

Dave and Gary looked at each other and left.

So...a bartender was having his friends on? Good joke.

The next day was Monday and Dave stopped to pick up the morning EXAMINER. The story?

Two bikies had been killed on the mainland and their bodies and bikes were being sent back to Hobart for the funeral.

Their bikes? Nortons.

Their boots? The kind you couldn't buy in Tasmania: Rossie's.

Stop in at the Exeter pub and ask for Charlie. Check the story out. We did.

THE HALLWAY

"It's in the hallway," she said. "I tell you it's in the hallway."

"Slow down, Alice! Slow down. What's in the hallway?"

"IT is! IT'S a something. A feeling. I couldn't walk past it. It made me stop. Besides, last night I felt it when I took a shower...and then there were the noises. Strange noises."

Conversations similar to this have been shared for generations at The Grange in Campbell Town.

Used for many years by the Education Department for seminars and meetings, the distinctive, sort-of-gothic brick building almost demands that it be haunted. The many chimney pots, small upstairs doors, old sealed windows, and immaculate English gardens lend an air of mystery to The Grange. Seen from a distance in the full moonlight, the viewer will be instantly reminded of a Nancy Drew or Hardy Brothers mystery novel. Everything is there for a perfect haunting.

And the ghostly appearances are almost perfect as well. Sometimes IT appears as a vapor. Sometimes IT is a wall through which one cannot pass. Sometimes IT is a ghostly sound. Sometimes IT is an odour.

We think that IT is a HE. Why a HE? We feel that the ghost of The Grange is old Dr. Valentine, the man who had the building erected in the middle 1800's. He was a unique man of several abilities: surgeon, architect, astronomer, politician, and even the establisher of a Turkish bath. Being a ghost could well be within his abilities, too.

Yet, Dr. Valentine, for all of his complexities, is said to have been a rather simple man. Of the many passions through which he comfortably moved, The Grange was an enduring one for him.

He would certainly approve of the educational weekends which take place regularly in his old home. You see, he was an educator as well.

But back to the experiences of the ghost of The Grange. There is one special room which 'he' seems to like more than others: the one directly over the kitchen. More than one person involved in adult education refuses to stay in that specific room. The authors once slept there while attending a seminar and have to give credence to 'strange sounds'. But, of course, those sounds would have to have been a possum...or the limb of a tree...or...?

Anyway, sightings or feelings of a ghost's presence in The Grange are most frequently experienced during an educational session when, for some reason or the other, a student will have to go to his or her room...perhaps for a notebook. THAT is the normal time for 'his' appearance or presentation. IF 'it' is Doc Valentine, he might just be checking out your credentials. The presence is most frequently encountered on the stairs or in the hallway.

But don't worry. No one has ever come to any harm in The Grange. If 'it', the ghost, is the Doctor, he is most assuredly friendly.

If you do experience the presence in the old home, you might also be interested to see Dr. Valentine's grave. The stone is at the right of the entrance to the first church on the left as you arrive from Launceston. Read his inscription.

Interestingly, you can see part of The Grange from his grave. We think he might be keeping an eye on the comings and goings at his old residence.

The Man with Four Daughters
The tin house at St. Helens.

The Hallway
Entally House, Hadspen

Norwich House, Norfolk Plains
The door.

The Hallway
*at The Grange,
Campbell Town.*

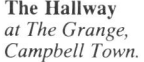

THE MAN WITH
FOUR DAUGHTERS

An abandoned old house in the middle of an old tin mining area seems an appropriate place for a haunting. And so it happened to two Tasmanian school teachers who, feeling near 'burn out', took a year off from work.

The children had left home a few years previously and retirement was still fifteen years away. Unless they took a long break soon, they both feared they would not be able to finish their jobs in the right frame of mind. They each had three months long service coming, and, if they rented out their home, were careful, AND went bush, they felt confident they would have a rewarding and relaxing year. Fishing. Bushwalking. Writing.

What the couple didn't plan for was dealing with the ghost of the tin house.

It was a nice enough shack to live in for a year: cheap, hidden in the bushes, electricity, even two fire places. No one had lived in the house for some time, so the two 'tired teachers' set about cleaning and painting and wall papering. Without the pressure of children and jobs, Gladys and Cliff felt like honeymooners again.

But once more, as in so many ghostly tales, the theme of 'happenings' is associated with renovations.

The first night in their snug little shack was decidedly crowded. Boxes were strewn everywhere in the little cottage. The two decided to bed down on a mattress in front of the fireplace. It was a bit cool, so they snuggled into their doona, the fire warming the tiny sitting room. Cliff opened a bottle of vintage red and they both felt very young again. There, in front of the crackling fire, they planned and dreamed and congratulated each other for being bold.

It had been a long day, and before half the bottle of red was consumed, they were both sleeping.

Cliff didn't know why he awoke. It was unusual for him. He was usually a very sound sleeper. Perhaps it was a possum on the roof. But no...it wasn't that. There were other people in the house! Cliff could see them. There were four middle aged women. They had just been crying and were obviously stressed. Some were carrying bouquets of flowers. None of the women saw Cliff and Gladys in front of the fire. In fact, it was as if Cliff were watching the happenings through a window.

But he was awake! He knew that! He tried to wake Gladys, but couldn't communicate with her. It was as if he were frozen in bed! Cliff wasn't fearful. He was more curious than anything.

As Cliff watched, the four women hugged each other and wept. One of them put flowers into vases and placed them around the house. Cliff remembered smelling lilacs. It was not springtime. The lady paid no attention to the two in bed. She moved THROUGH them.

About that time, children came into the house. Cliff couldn't remember any noise, but he knew they were being noisy...but there WAS no noise.

The ladies prepared tea in the small kitchen, but space didn't seem to be a problem. The screen door slammed shut without a sound! But there WAS no screen door.

It was then that Cliff realized what he was watching: a family get-together after a funeral. But why in their little old mining shack?

Almost laconically, Cliff watched the party develop. He came to like two of the women, dislike one, and feel indifferent to another. They were sisters, that was obvious; big lumpy women they were.

As suddenly as the images had appeared to Cliff, they now disappeared...fttttt!

Now Cliff could move. He was under the doona with Gladys, and the fire still had embers. He WAS awake! He awakened Gladys and told her everything he had seen. They agreed that something strange had happened and huddled together until sleep overcame them again.

Next morning, Cliff told Gladys that he had to go to the cemetery to see 'something'. He didn't know what...or why. Upon arriving in the graveyard, Cliff immediately walked to one of the markers. "I think this is the one," he said. He had never been in the graveyard before, and the name on the stone meant nothing to either of them. It read, 'Groves'.

Time passed and the images of the first night were fairly well forgotten after the initial sensation. It was almost time to move back to Hobart and take up their teaching careers again. They had become recharged.

Time for one more fishing sojourn down on the wharf. The bream were running, he had heard. There Cliff and Gladys – very gregarious people that they were – struck up a conversation with an old retired local. They exchanged pleasantries and the old man asked, "Where do you live? Seen you around here for some time now."

Cliff told him.

"Oh, I heard that there were some new people in the old Groves' place. You know, that place is haunted. Been that way for years."

Cliff gulped. "Know anything about it? I mean the haunting?"

"Not much. Only that I went to school with the youngest of the girls. Was real sweet on her too. She was a beauty."

"ONE of the girls?" Cliff continued. He could feel himself flush.

"Yeah, old Groves had four daughters. Real close family. Wonder whatever came of them? They left town...oh...forty years ago."

THE GHOST OF THE BALL AND CHAIN

When next you are dining in the Ball and Chain (Salamanca Place, Hobart), look again if you see someone sitting alone in the corner booth beside the kitchen door. The 'person' may well be Charlie the Ghost.

Charlie, they say, likes to sit in his corner seat when the restaurant is fairly empty. Nadia thought he was a late lunch customer when she came to work at 5 p.m. Looking back, she admits he was a little unusual. His yellow and green attire didn't seem to fit the expected dress of the middle-aged man he appeared to be. Nor did he seem to respond to her greeting as she passed by on her way to the kitchen. (It may be noted here that convict clothing could, in the half-light, be construed as yellow and green.)

But when Nadia mentioned his presence to the kitchen staff, she was told that the last lunch customers had left two hours before. Sure enough, when she returned to set up the tables, the corner seat was empty. Yet no one could have departed...she had locked the street door.

Other employees of the Ball and Chain report having seen Charlie...always in the same seat in the corner...always when no one else is there. It is also a strange thing that customers don't often sit in Charlie's corner seat. And some who do report feeling 'something' pull the food from their hands. (Perhaps some legs are being pulled as well!)

And why is it that the panels which form the back of Charlie's seat have sometimes been pulled apart as if by the weight of someone sitting there...when nobody has?

Next time you dine at the Ball and Chain, ask about Charlie...or, better still, sit in his seat. But hang on to your fork!

OLD WREST POINT STAIRCASE

The history of Wrest Point, Hobart, would explain many a ghostly apparition. The present mood of rest, relaxation, and revelry is far different from the mood of the early 1800's. For Wrest Point was then Gibbet Point, the site of executions and of bodies left to rot for public view.

The original house was built by Norfolk Islander, Thomas Chaffey, when hangings still took place on Gibbet Point. Perhaps the retail potential of the site outweighed the disadvantages of proximity to the place of execution. Or perhaps Thomas Chaffey enjoyed the spectacle. His son, David, certainly enjoyed the Long Beach races. David also saw there was money to be made. So he built Traveller's Rest as a watering hole for thirsty race goers.

Not only did Traveller's Rest fortify race goers; it became the haunt of smugglers.

Public hangings...fortunes lost and won...smugglers. No wonder the house built by David Dunkley on the site of Gibbet Point was said to be haunted. He complained about voices when there were no people...he heard footsteps when no one was there. Smugglers' tunnels? Perhaps. People said they existed.

The sounds continued after Dunkley's death, except now they were believed to be the ghost of Dunkley himself. Footsteps...voices...apparitions. At last it was too much. In 1900, Mr. Plowman, the current owner, had Dunkley's house demolished and built a new house in its place. He called it St. Helen's.

The footsteps ceased. The voices were silent. Perhaps the smugglers' tunnels had been filled in.

Yet there are those who still report seeing an apparition on the stairs of St. Helen's. A smuggler? A hanged convict?

THE MOURNFUL MUSIC OF WANSTEAD

You have probably admired the lovely old Georgian-cum-Australian Colonial house many times as you have driven by on the Midlands Highway. Its gracious, geometrical lines are pleasing to view.

Perhaps with its age and interesting history you might also expect to see a ghost or two...perhaps that of a convict or bushranger. Richard Willis, who built Wanstead c1827, was well known for his pursuit and capture of runaways and outlaws. Indeed, Richard's original grant of 2,000 acres was increased to 8,000 as a reward for his daring.

Yet Wanstead is not known for a ghost you can see. Instead, it is known for the ghost you can HEAR. The sound is that of music...lovely piano music...wistful and sad. Yet no human hand plays the mournful notes. No one is seated at a piano. No radio plays.

Legend has it that the music is the haunting sound of Richard's daughter as she mourns the violent loss of her fiancee. It is said she turned to the piano for solace...hence the melancholy tunes which speak of her sad soul. Is this daughter the Marianne Serjeantson (nee Willis) whose husband is documented to have been shot dead whilst riding the boundary in search of lost cattle? It is known that her captain husband's body was returned to Wanstead. Did she, too, mourn her loss in music?

Are they two separate stories? Or are they the same...the one set in history, the other moulded by time and the oral tradition? Be that as it may, there are many who speak of the mournful music of Wanstead...and of the sad soul which plays those notes.

The Mournful Music of Wanstead
Wanstead, Campbell Town.

The Light in the Brewery Window
Shouten House where the light shines.
Swansea.

THE FLOGGING GHOST OF RICHMOND BRIDGE

Walk across Richmond Bridge on a foggy night and perhaps you will see the ghost of Groover the Flagellator. Sometimes, they say, he is headless. Always he is seen as the mist rises from the river, curls across the bridge, and creeps up into the town.

For it was on such a night that Groover the Flagellator was murdered. Groover was one of the overseers of the convict work gangs which built the bridge...and he was probably the most hated. Not content to see the convicts act as beasts of burden as they hauled stone, he would often add his own substantial weight to the carts as they were pulled up hill from the quarry. And if he imagined the pace was too slow, he enjoyed picking strips of flesh from the convicts' backs. Needless to say, Groover was a marked man.

Richmond Bridge was almost completed when Groover's time came. It was late. The night was dark. The fog had settled. As Groover walked across the bridge, he was followed by some of the men who he had tormented. He was struck down. When the fog lifted, his body was discovered on the bank below.

It is not known whether anyone was charged with Groover's murder. The fact that his unappeased soul still walks the bridge would suggest not...But if you want to verify the truth of Groover's ghost, why not stand on Richmond Bridge next time the night is foggy?

THE DRUNKEN HAG OF CAMPBELL TOWN

The word 'hag' brings visions of a skinny, broken-toothed old woman with bony fingers and a maddened laugh. And such a hag is said to haunt the northern approach to Campbell Town...not too far from the graveyard.

The story goes that she was a convict known for her drinking and carousing. As she grew older, she became madder. Children were warned to stay away from her. Even grown men gave her a wide berth as she shouted abuse and vilifications on the edge of town.

Usually she was drunk. Always she was angry.

She was both drunk and angry on the day she died. She was in her usual place on the northern end of town. What made her start to cross the road is not recorded. Perhaps she simply wanted the sunny side of the street. Perhaps she had seen someone coming on the other side. No matter the reason, she staggered into the path of a coach and was killed.

People still report the sudden appearance of an old hag in the path of their vehicle as they approach Campbell Town. The apparition shakes its fist and mouths abuse...then disappears.

So, on your next journey north...or south...the old hag of Campbell Town might be another good reason for slowing down as you approach the town.

THE HAUNTED ROAD

For the most part, the road from Sorell to Richmond follows the original convict road. It is a lovely, peaceful lane as it winds through gentle hills and pastoral countryside from one old colonial settlement to the other. As you drive the narrow road on a warm, sunny day, thoughts of tragic happenings and possible hauntings will probably be far from your mind.

Yet, there are those who swear that a particular spot on that very road is haunted. Horses shy away as they pass the spot. Dogs inexplicably growl and cringe...for no reason, so their owners say. Some passersby have reported an overwhelming feeling of uneasiness – even dread – so much so that their legs would not move and their hair stood on end.

Why? The reason (so the legend goes) dates back to the old days of convicts and bushrangers...a time of violence and crime. And the crime that was committed on this particular spot was one of the worst. A young female settler was on her way home. It was late in the afternoon. The sun was setting and she was hurrying to reach her destination before dark. Had she heard of the convict who had recently escaped? That we do not know.

The spot where the convict was hiding was where the road dipped into a small hollow, and where some bushes grew close to the side. He waited, listening to her approaching footsteps, and as she came close, he sprang. The poor woman began to run in terror, but too late. She was grappled to the ground, raped and strangled...then (as now) a heinous crime. Next day, her body was found in the long grass beside the road.

No wonder horses, dogs, and people shy at the spot, but that is not the end of the story. Some years later a second murder is said to have occurred on the very same spot...or was it a murder? A young man by the name of Frazer had been out hunting with friends. It was a dark night and the party had separated. Suddenly there was a terrified scream...an undeniable scream for help.

No one doubted that something terrible had happened, but it took Mr. Frazer's friends some time to find him. His eyes were bulging in terror. His face was contorted. He still seemed to be staring at an indescribably horrible vision. But he was dead...half-draped, half-clinging to the top rail of the fence...on almost the exact spot where the young woman's body had been found.

So, next time you take the car from Sorell to Richmond, drive slowly. Perhaps you will find the tragic spot. Or better still, take your bicycle...or walk.

But be careful. Don't linger!

JOHN BATMAN'S GHOST?

Georgetown is, arguably, Australia's oldest village, and a number of the old buildings still remain. Some of the structures are grand, such as the Grove (once the residence of Matthew Curling Friend and now a restaurant). Others are charming workers' cottages which overlook the Tamar River.

One of the oldest and grandest buildings is the former Little Queen Inn. Situated close to the waterfront, this venerable building could tell many a tale of colonial days. But the snorting of horses, the clatter of coaches, the sounds of merriment from the bar, are memories now. The Little Queen Inn has retired from its days as watering hole for sailors and guest house for travellers.

Yet there are those who claim that something of the old days still remains. Like the sound of footsteps entering the front door and proceeding up the hall...then ascending the stairs and proceeding to the maid's room. Then the sound of baggage being moved and dragged across the floor. Inexplicable sounds of an unknown origin. Many times the source of the sounds...the footsteps, the hauling of boxes...has been investigated by subsequent residents, and no one was there.

Rats in the attic? Possums in the roof? Perhaps. But how does one explain the appearance of a tall, imposing man dressed in colonial clothing at the top of the stairs? The owners of forty years ago declared that the apparition looked down at them long enough for them to remember his fawn-coloured coat, his top hat, his striking resemblance to pictures of John Batman. Indeed, it seemed as though he was about to speak, when he...disappeared!

There is no record of John Batman staying at Little Queen Inn, but it is very possible that he did...perhaps on his way to 'found' Melbourne, or on one of his many journeys in old Van Diemen's Land. Perhaps the apparition at the top of the stairs WAS John Batman...

Perhaps the footsteps and the sounds of baggage are his too. Or perhaps they are merely those of an old time traveller coming back to claim lost luggage.

"A QUARTER PAST ELEVEN"

Lady Binney, wife of Governor Binney, was not one to believe in ghosts. She was a strong-minded lady of solid reputation who would expect to find a logical explanation for things that might seem strange.

For this reason, she at first took little notice of the muffled voices, the low moans, the echoing footsteps. After all, Government House is a very old building with numerous corridors. The sandstone construction and thick walls could reflect and distort sound from one end of the building to the other...couldn't they?

But as Lady Binney became more acquainted with Government House and with those who worked there, the sounds became less and less explicable. Why footsteps when she was sure the building was empty? Why voices when she knew no one was there? And there was that particular voice, distinct and memorable: "It's a quarter past eleven". Always the same voice. Always the same words. "It's a quarter past eleven".

Governor and Lady Binney left Government House many years ago. It is not known whether subsequent governors and their ladies have heard the same sounds. However, as damp courses are restored and stones are replaced, will the ghosts be disturbed?

Will 'it's a quarter to eleven' be heard again?

THE SWINGING DOOR OF VALLEYFIELD

Swinging doors, muffled voices, and footsteps seem to be the most frequent phenomena associated with ghost tales. In fact, no ghost tale would be quite complete without one or more of them.

Valleyfield (not far from New Norfolk) has its swinging door. It is a strong door with a good latch...yet for some unknown reason it swings open. Being an inside door which leads to bedrooms, wind can't be the answer. Besides, it would take a very strong wind to blow open such a heavy construction. Why, then, is the door found to be open when it has recently been closed?

Perhaps the answer lies in the fact that the inside door was once an outside door facing an exterior stairway; for Valleyfield was once the King's Head Inn...a place of good times and conviviality. But times WEREN'T always good in old Van Diemen's Land. It was also an era of bushrangers, criminals, and escaped convicts. Settlers lived in fear, especially when a desperate escapee was known to be at large.

The year was 1826. Matthew Brady, one of Tasmania's most ruthless bushrangers, was known to be in the area. When the landlord of the King's Head Inn heard sounds of someone opening the window...climbing over the sill...jumping softly to the floor...he assumed a holdup. He grabbed his gun and cocked it. Brady was in his sights. He fired. The bushranger dropped to the floor, dead. The landlord had protected his property.

But had he? As he shone the lantern onto the face of the dead man, he found it was not Brady. It was his own son! The young man had apparently been out on a jaunt and was trying to sneak in.

Is the phenomenon of the swinging door explained by the ghost of the returning son? Or is it caused by the spirit of an anguished father returning to the scene of personal tragedy?

THE STRANGLED DOG OF SASSAFRAS

The house has gone now, but the tale remains. It is a macabre story of murder by strangling...first of man, then of dog.

The events took place in a house near Sassafras, close to Paramatta Creek. The old man who once occupied the house was known to be a miser. He had his money hidden somewhere in the house -- under the floor, inside his mattress, up the chimney. Somewhere. Not surprisingly, the old man and his money became the target of a thief. The old man was strangled. It is not known whether his cache was discovered.

From that time on the house remained empty, falling into disrepair. Neighbours avoided it. There was an 'evil presence', they said. "Don't go near it," they warned.

One day a visitor came to the area. Being a strong-minded person who didn't believe in ghosts, he scoffed at the story. "I'll prove it's not haunted," he bragged. "I'll spend the night there." So, taking his lantern and his dog, he entered the house.

With his dog at his side, he waited for something to happen. All was quiet. Hours seemed to pass. He was getting bored...and cold. He was just deciding to go home, when, suddenly, for no reason, the lantern went out. At the same time, his dog began to bark, then snarl. It was attacking something in the room! The sounds of struggle continued, but, try as he would, the lantern wouldn't light. Soon the ferocious sounds of the dog turned to desperate yelps, then to a pitiful whine.

When the lantern was finally lit, the dog was dead. Its body lay in the corner...STRANGLED! Like the old miser!

Needless to say, the now-believing ghost hunter fled. We don't know if he ever returned to claim his dog. Somehow, we doubt it.

BOTHWELL'S GREY LADY

Ladies are frequently the subject of ghost tales – the lady in white, the lady in blue, the lady in serving wench's dress. But it is the Grey Lady who makes her appearance in 'Wentworth', Bothwell.

The Grey Lady has been seen by numerous people. Perhaps the most notable was the Anglican Bishop back in the days when 'Wentworth' was 'the Rectory'. The Reverend Bishop was doing his pastoral rounds, and where better to find accommodation than in the charming midlands town of Bothwell with its lovely village green? And, of course, there was to be a 'gathering'. The most notable people from the district had been invited, and that meant formal dress.

The Bishop always did have trouble with his clerical collar, but tonight it was worse than usual. He just couldn't seem to fit the notch in his collar to the stud on his shirt. Try as he would, they wouldn't match. (Perhaps he was missing the help of his wife!)

When the dinner bell rang, he was STILL fumbling with his collar. Not wanting to be late, he glanced into the mirror – to find someone standing behind him. That someone was a lady: a lady with a pale, gentle face. A kind-looking lady. A lady in grey. "Yes, I'll be right down," he said, thinking she was summoning him for tea.

Later on that evening, the Bishop happened to ask about the Grey Lady. It seemed strange to him that she wasn't among the guests. "Oh, you've seen our Grey Lady, have you?" his host replied. "She appears quite frequently."

We are sure that Bothwell has other ghosts, too. The very town is haunted with its convict past, its tales of the bushranger, Martin Cash...its old graveyards. Among them is the Grey Lady of Wentworth who still shows her face from time to time (so the story goes).

A CHINESE GHOST

Strange things seem to happen around Weldborough. Lights shine where no lights should be. Sometimes people appear and then vanish. The whole area seems to languish in times gone by...of men toiling for tin, of poor miner's huts, of women and children...of Chinese labourers. For, not long ago, Weldborough, Blue Tiers, and Gould's Country were thought to be where fortunes could be made – in more ways than one.

Among the Chinese population was a man who was rumoured to have 'struck it rich' through selling lottery tickets. And, of course (so people said), he had his money hidden somewhere. After all, he was clever, hard working, and lucky...and he was saving up for the journey home. Perhaps inevitably (for the time and place), the Chinese man was murdered. The year was about 1852.

At night, and for years after, the mining population of Weldborough would not pass the spot where the murder took place. Today, some people still recall the line of people waiting on the roadside for daylight to break.

Does the murder of the Chinese lottery seller have something to do with the strange light which appears on a nearby hill...a light which cannot be explained? Or did the victim find peace at last when his bones were returned to his ancestoral home? Who knows?

WILLIAM RUMNEY NEVER DID WANT TO LEAVE HOME

As William Rumney built his home near Seven Mile Beach, he felt it was the best thing he had ever done or was ever likely to do. For, 160 years later, 'Acton' is still a grand house, and Seven Mile Beach has become a very desirable place to live. Little wonder that William viewed the finished product with a grateful heart and vowed that this would be where he would live his life and end his days.

William led a peaceful and satisfying life. He took care of his farm. He went hunting. He strolled on the beach. He enjoyed his home. He went to church. But, as it does for all of us, William Rumney's time came. It happened one day after church. He suffered a heart attack and died. He was mourned, eulogized, and buried.

But did William Rumney ever leave home? "Who is the old gentleman I saw in the drawing room?" people sometimes ask. "He was standing near the fireplace. He looked...well...unusual. You see, he was dressed in colonial clothes." The 'old gentleman' never speaks, and, of course, when they go back to investigate, there is no one there.

Perhaps old Bill Rumney is still at 'Acton'. For, who hasn't built a home they love and said, "I never want to leave"?

THE GHOST OF GIBBET HILL

Have you ever felt the hair on your neck rise as you drive by Gibbet Hill? If so, you are one of the many who have. And if you have driven the Midlands Highway by night, perhaps you are one of the few who have seen a figure walking on the road...yes, ON the road. Right in the path of your car. A figure which ignores the sound of your urgent horn. Too late! You brake. For an instant you catch sight of a blank, expressionless face in the glare of the lights. Then you pass over it, or through it, or both. Or has it passed over or through you?

If such has been your experience, you were probably on that part of the highway just north of Perth – a place which came to be known as Gibbet Hill because of the convicted criminals who were left to hang there. And the apparition you saw was probably the ghost of an escaped prisoner named Mackay.

The year was 1837, in the days of J.E. Cox's mail coach. The road between Hobart and Launceston was rough and the going was slow. Not only did the coach carry the royal mail, it also carried passengers...sometimes wealthy ones. That is why escaped convict Mackay lay in ambush. He had been told that wealthy Henry Reed (landlord of the Cornwall Hotel, Launceston) would ride the coach that day.

But, for whatever reason (or, as some would say, 'as Fate would have it'), Reed had arranged for James Wilson to make the journey in his place. As the mail coach toiled up Gibbet Hill, Mackay sprang from his hiding place, stopped the coach, and shot the man he thought was Reed. Enraged at discovering his mistake, Mackay then clubbed the wounded Wilson to death. Eventually, Mackay was apprehended, tried, and found guilty. Because of the callousness of his crime, he was sentenced to be hanged in chains and gibbeted at the scene of the murder.

It was Henry Reed who played a major role in releasing Mackay's decaying body from its bonds. In the autumn of the same year, Reed was travelling the Midlands Highway, and, passing Gibbet Hill, he was horrified by the gruesome spectacle of Mackay's remains. He fell to his knees, praying to God for the sinner's soul...and when he returned to Launceston, he persuaded the authorities to remove the gruesome sight.

So, Mackay's body was finally put to rest...but was his soul? Or is the ghost of Gibbet Hill the ghost of Wilson, still haunting the spot where he was clubbed? Or is it Reed's spirit, still tormented by the sight of the convict's putrid body? Or do Mackay, Wilson, and Reed – all three – still reenact those anguished moments?

(Dennis Hodgkinson)

THE PHANTOM OF THE PRINCESS THEATRE

Most hauntings in Tasmania seem to be associated with the early days, but the Phantom of the Princess Theatre (Launceston) is a recent phenomenon. The strange happenings began in 1972, and seem to be associated with the fact that the Princess is no longer used exclusively for live theatre.

John still cannot explain the distinct sound of scratching – like the scratching of fingernails across the baffle boards – during the screening of the Walking Club's 'Do You Know Tasmania'.

The noise was not on the sound track. Nor was it produced by the sound apparatus. Nor could anyone interfere with the baffle boards without being seen. Because the film was screened by back projection, John would have known had someone been on stage.

Gary still puzzles over the sudden change in temperature which occurred in the projection box during the screening of 'The Amityville Horror' – a film depicting the horrendous haunting of a house. Why, when the powerful arc lights reach temperatures of 2,000 degrees, did it become so cold that Gary had to turn on the electric heater?

The strange happenings don't end with mysterious scratchings and sudden chills. There was the sound of footsteps – heavy footsteps – along the catwalk used by scene painters. There is the time when the air became so cold that it seemed as though the temperature had dropped 15 degrees in five minutes. Yet John had removed his jumper only moments before. After all, nailing battens is very sweaty work.

But the strangest occurrence of all was when both Gary and John arrived for work one morning. Of course, the theatre was locked. How, then, had someone been able to enter? They could hear the sounds of the piano playing quite distinctly from where they were standing outside the stage door. Hoping to surprise the intruder, they decided to enter by the front door instead. As they passed into the pitch-dark building, the music continued. No light came from the stage where the piano stood...yet the playing went on. But, as the house lights came up, the music stopped abruptly. The theatre was silent. The stage was empty. When they searched the building, they heard nothing and saw no one. Nor could they explain why the lid of the keyboard was down, yet there had been no sound of it closing.

Who is the Phantom of the Princess Theatre? Someone who worked there? Someone involved in live theatre? Someone who doesn't like films?...

When next you visit the Princess, take a few moments to examine the Max Oldaker collection in the dress circle foyer. Max was a live theatre man through and through, understudy to Rex Harrison, veteran of Drury Lane. He was also a veteran of the Princess Theatre. Max died in Launceston in 1970. The signed photographs, the music, the scripts are proof of his dedication.

Is Max the Phantom of the Princess Theatre?

(Dennis Hodgkinson)

MR. ELLIS' FRIENDLY GHOST

Ask Mr. Ellis of Waverley whether he believes in ghosts and he will answer with a spontaneous 'yes'. "What's more," he will probably continue, " they're...well...they're sort of friends of mine. You see, I've lived with two of them. Or it could be the same one. I'm not really sure."

Mr. Ellis first became acquainted with ghosts when he lived in My Street. The house was old – perhaps over 100 years. "I saw him several times," Mr. Ellis explained over a cuppa. "He would come in at the front door, walk along the passage, and go out at the back. If the door was locked, he'd unlock it." Mr. Ellis paused to stir his cup. "I reckon he was a good bloke, though," he continued. "He never did any of us any harm. And he had a good, heavy tread – as if he knew exactly what he was about. He sounded 'solid'."

Mr. Ellis paused again, and we sat for a moment wondering whether there was more to the story. But we didn't have to wait for long. "This place is haunted, too," he went on. We looked around the kitchen of the 32 year-old Commission home. It didn't seem to qualify for spooks. "We hear him shuffling around at night...slowly. As though he's looking for something. Not like before. This place is carpeted, you know. Can't hear him like in the other one.

"Well, one day one of the daughters had her boyfriend over for the night. 'Mind the spooks,' I warned him as he was about to doss down on the couch. I went to bed myself, but it didn't seem too long before the boyfriend was at the bedroom door. 'Can't sleep for that ***!!## ghost,' he muttered. 'Well, wrap a blanket round your head,' I said.'"

Mr. Ellis paused again to take a final sip. There was the hint of a twinkle in his eye. "Now I know our spook's a friendly ghost," he went on, "there's only two things that bother me. The first is, if he's up all night, where on earth does he go all day?" Mr. Ellis got up to collect our mugs. Then, grinning, he turned to us. "The second is, why ever won't he stop for a cup of tea? I ask him often enough."

(Dennis Hodgkinson)

THE RESTLESS SOUL OF PENQUITE
or
THE CASE OF THE FOOTLESS TRACKS

If you see a tall man with hunched shoulders taking a short cut across the land between Penquite Road and the North Esk River (Launceston), look again. It might be the Restless Soul of Penquite. Or, if your eyes tell you that the grass is being trampled by invisible feet, don't jump to the conclusion that you are going 'round the bend'. Others have witnessed those footless tracks.

One man, who grew up in the area, has had several such experiences. The first occurred around May in 1971 when he was a young boy. He was letting off some crackers with a friend, when, suddenly, they both saw footsteps moving through the fallen leaves...leaving behind a trail of prints where no one had been! Of course, both boys were terrified. One took to his heels. The other, too petrified to move, watched as the bodiless steps continued through the leaves and disappeared over the fence on the farthest side.

The same boy has also seen the Restless Soul of Penquite several times. Usually the sighting was from a distance, but in 1983 it came almost close enough to touch – and certainly close enough for the boy to observe some startling features. The face was blotched as though it had been badly burned. The ears were lobeless, as though they had been 'melted'. Yet the figure was the same one he had seen before...about 6'2", with slumping walk. And as the figure passed him, it was as though the door of some huge freezing chamber had opened to emit a flood of sub-zero air. Where did the boy see the apparition? On the spot of the footless tracks!

On another occasion, the young boy was playing in the paddock with his pet cat. As the figure appeared on the other side of the field, the cat froze, its back arched, its hair on end. As the figure approached, the cat took off.

Others have seen the Restless Soul of Penquite: the boy's mother, some of the neighbours. And others have seen the footless tracks...

Like the man, who (sometime in the 1930's) was employed to clear the block of land. While he was busy working, he was astonished to see the long grass which he was cutting being trampled by invisible feet. Unable to deny what his own eyes saw, he ran away. Of course, he never went back.

...Would you?

(Dennis Hodgkinson)

THE HAUNTED CELL

The old Supreme Court in Launceston stood at the corner of Wellington and Paterson Streets. Part of the complex were the remand cells where prisoners were held. Although the site has been occupied by TAFE (formerly the Launceston Technical College) since the 1920's, stories are still told of a notorious cell which even the most hardened criminals feared.

The story is simple. A woman prisoner was awaiting trial. She was so terrified of appearing in court that, in desperation, she hung herself. From that time on, the cell she had occupied became a place of terror.

Prisoners who were kept there overnight were often found next morning in a state of near madness. Most pleaded to be moved to a different cell. It was always the same story. The room was haunted...by a deranged woman. She terrorized them the whole night. The possibility of all the prisoners being acquainted with the story beforehand was slight. Even the most sceptical police officers were convinced there was something bad inside those walls.

The old Court House cells have since been demolished, and the woman's ghost is gone. However, at the time of their demolition 'The Examiner' (August 1936) reported that even the most confirmed disbeliever would find it difficult to explain the haunting. We wonder what the demolition gang found.

(Dennis Hodgkinson)

CALUMET

The residents of Calumet say they are used to their ghost, and that if he really wants to live in the dungeon, he's welcome!

The house, one of Hobart's old mansions, has recently been divided into pleasant apartments. It is the residents of the basement flats who are most acquainted with Calumet's ghost. Frequently, when relaxing quietly in their living rooms, they hear the sound of footsteps descending the wooden stairs to the corridor outside. They are soft footsteps, as though the person is wearing rubber-soled shoes.

At first, when the footsteps stopped outside, the residents would wait for someone to knock. It was as though that someone were deciding which door to choose. But the expected knock never came. At first, the occupants would open the door, expecting to find a visitor outside. But no one was there. They have now almost come to take the footsteps for granted...after all, whatever it is has done no harm.

There are two outside doors on the basement floor of Calumet. One leads to the two apartments. The other gives entry to the disused dungeon below. It is dark and spooky...and full of spiders. It's not a place anyone would want to go...

Except a ghost!

THE GHOST OF MRS. BUSCOMBE

It seems that Mrs. Buscombe still likes a chat! And it also seems that she is still looking for those jewels she hid somewhere.

The story goes . . . The Buscombes built a grand, two-storey, colonial house just outside Richmond on the road to Sorell. They called it 'Prospect'. The Buscombes also owned property in Richmond and were involved in a number of local businesses. When Mr. Buscombe died, his wife and sons continued to live in the house.

Evidently, the relationship between Mrs. Buscombe and her sons was not perfect. Or perhaps as she got older she became distrustful...and forgetful. Anyway, when their business began to go bad, Mrs. Buscombe decided to hide her jewels. Where she hid them no one knows. Nor could Mrs. Buscombe herself remember. Although subsequent occupants of the house have searched, they have never been found.

Time passes. Mrs. Buscombe joined her husband in Richmond's Anglican graveyard. 'Prospect' was sold. Others moved in – and out. Eventually the old house was converted to a restaurant. And recently (and fittingly) the descendants of the original Buscombes have bought the house.

But throughout 'Prospect's' history, ghosts have been rumoured. The first account dates to the end of last century. A young eighteen year-old woman was spending her first night in one of the upstairs rooms, when, suddenly, she was awakened. Standing above her was a terrifying SOMETHING – it had two holes for eyes and it was leaning over her bed. Petrified beyond moving, she spent the rest of the night with the covers over her head. Not surprisingly, she refused to sleep in that room again.

Recent reports of ghostly meetings are of a happier nature. The figure of a woman dressed in old-time clothing and a white, frilly cap is sometimes seen wandering the house. She most frequently appears on the cellar stairs. Sometimes she is sitting as though trying to remember. At others she is descending, as though searching. And sometimes she is mumbling to herself.

A retired air-traffic controller – he was a trained observer and not prone to flights of fancy – swore to a meeting with the ghost of Mrs. Buscombe on the cellar stairs. She was coming up and he was going down. She smiled, and they sat down together and had a pleasant chat. Perhaps, as he too was a Buscombe, she wanted to catch up on family news.

So, when next you are visiting historical Richmond, call into Prospect House for a Plowman's Lunch or a Devonshire Tea. Ask after Mrs. Buscombe. As possibly Tasmania's only talking ghost, she may well be wanting to chat.

Mrs. Buscombe's grave, Richmond.

Mrs. Buscombe's stairs,
Prospect House, Richmond.

GUNSHOTS AND BLUE SMOKE
AT SHERWIN

Unlike most haunted houses, Sherwin is not particularly old...yet weird things happen there. The inexplicable occurrences are like the reenactment of a duel...or could it be a battle...or a murder?

When young Claudette moved in with her Persian cat, she immediately began seeing...and hearing...and smelling strange things: thumps as though someone were falling off a chair; creakings as though someone were walking in the corridor outside; sharp explosions as though someone had just fired a shot. Then a blue mist would appear and spread through the room – a blue mist like the smoke from an old-fashioned gun. And then there was the smell of gunpowder.

At first Claudette was scared, but as the happenings continued with no harm to her, she decided not to be alarmed. Whatever the explanation, there seemed to be no malice. And after two years, it all seemed quite normal.

When Claudette's two sisters came to share the house, they too witnessed the sounds, the blue smoke...even the acrid smell. But no bullet holes appeared in the walls. No body was found. No newspapers reported persons missing or dead.

One day, the girls' parents – who lived in another part of the state – happened to mention the strange occurrences to a friend. He was a bushman with an intimate knowledge of local folklore. When informed that Sherwin is near Port Sorell, he asked for more details. "Why!" he exclaimed. "It must have been built on Parker's Track!"

An investigation of the old records revealed the story: The year was 1831. The date was August 31st. The time was the reign of Governor Arthur. It happened that Captain Bartholomew B. Thomas (who had taken over North Down at Port Sorell) and James Parker (his faithful servant) were superintending supplies that had been shipped in from Launceston. Having already established friendly relationships with the local Aborigines, they were keen to come to terms with the disgruntled and hostile Big River tribe who had just moved into the area.

Confident that he could come to peaceful terms with the new-comers, Captain Thomas (accompanied by Parker, and against his advice) set out on foot to parley with them. On Parker's insistence, they were armed with a double-barreled gun.

At first the Aborigines seemed friendly as they walked on either side of the two men. All seemed well...so far. But when about two miles into the bush, the Aborigines rushed Parker, violently grabbing his gun and striking him to unconsciousness with their waddies. Both James Parker and Captain B. Thomas were speared to death.

Sherwin – where Claudette and her two sisters experienced the ghostly happenings – is built on what today is still known as 'Parker's Track'. The house is situated on or near to the place of the killings.

It seems that James Parker, or Captain Thomas – or both – are still trying to set the story 'right'.

(Dennis Hodgkinson)

THE GHOSTS OF ENTALLY HOUSE

Entally House is one of the oldest pioneer colonial homes in Australia, and it seems that it is haunted by more than one ghost. Built c1820 by Thomas Reiby, and now open to visitors, it has quite a history – much of it supernatural.

For a start, numerous people have heard the puzzling noise of a wheelbarrow being pushed across cobblestones. Many have been frightened by the sound, especially as there are no cobblestones and as the gardener's wheelbarrow is locked in the shed. However, there is an explanation. The story is that a man fell from his horse while riding near the old homestead. Whether he was already dead when he was wheeled to Entally is not known. Perhaps he died in the house. What we know is that wheelbarrows of colonial times were much larger and longer than they are now!

Then there is the story of the Indian servant. The first known sighting of this colourful spook occurred sometime in the 1940's. A young female was visiting the house. Feeling tired one afternoon, she announced she was going to take a nap and retired to her room in the attic. She hadn't been gone long, however, before she returned – somewhat wide-eyed and pale. Pressed to explain what had frightened her, she told of an apparition which had entered her room and had stood by her bed. He was a black man, she said. He was wearing bright clothing, she said. The garments were some strange Asian costume, she said. When she tried to speak to her colourful visitor, he vanished.

...Does the colourful apparition have a connection with the fact that Thomas Reiby spent time in India and, evidently, brought back some Indian servants?

Maryanne has her own story to tell. She was alone in the house and decided to do some vacuuming. The corridors of Entally are many and long. It would have been quite possible for someone to have entered the house through one of the doors...and to have approached Maryanne from behind. So, when Maryanne sensed someone standing over her shoulder, she wasn't too surprised. It was probably a friend come to visit. Not only could she FEEL the presence, she could see the shape of someone from the corner of her eye. Yet, when she turned to speak, the shape disappeared.

That is not the end of Maryanne's story. A few weeks later she was again vacuuming. She had finished cleaning downstairs and was in the process of carrying the cleaner up to the second floor. While ascending the stairs, she distinctly felt two hands touch her firmly on the head. As she tried to take the next step, the touch became even stronger. She was forced to stop! Of course, it was a friend playing a trick. Yet, when she looked around, no one was there!

Other weird things happen in Entally House. Who can explain the case of the opening clock face? Many times it is found to be unhinged when it is known to have been shut. And what about those blue, disapproving eyes of the old lady as you climb the stairs? And recently a clock which has not worked for years has begun to chime at various, unexpected times.

Neither Maryanne nor the other workers at Entally house are particularly worried about the ghosts. But it is no wonder that those who manage the mansion go home at night!

The Ghosts of Entally House
The upstairs bedroom.

Norwich House, Norfolk Plains
Stairs to the Attic.

RATTESKELLAR

The year was 1958. The young woman was spending her first weekend in the home of her fiancee's parents. The group – father, mother, son, and prospective daughter-in-law – were having tea in the kitchen of the old Georgian farmhouse overlooking the river. (The kitchen was a later 'lean to' addition to the original building – a rendered, convict brick construction in precise, uncompromising geometry.)

The two young lovers were on their way to a dance, and the young woman had purchased a dress for the occasion. It was still wrapped in brown paper in the spare room upstairs – a lovely, simple princess line in embossed taffeta. "Why don't you bring it down?" the young man suggested. He was eager to show off his latest girlfriend.

It was almost dusk outside, but inside the house it was almost dark. The young woman hurried along the passage towards the stairs. She could see them now – the mother, the father, and the young man – watching as she waltzed into the kitchen. She would be a vision in pink: slim waist, full bust, and long hair in French role. She had seldom been admired before. She was excited...and apprehensive, too.

Her mind was filled with the contents of the brown paper parcel, the vision of herself in pink, and the faces of those in the kitchen. She wasn't even aware of the stairs...until she reached the attic landing. Suddenly she stopped. It was gloomy above, but SOMEONE was there. She could see the unmistakable figure of a person looking down at her. Who? It must be the young man's father. But how? She had left him in the kitchen. They were ALL in the kitchen.

She spoke, but the figure neither moved nor answered. She spoke again, but still no answer. She stayed where she was, looking up at the figure which stood looking down at her. She COULDN'T move. Perhaps IT couldn't, either. Was it about to speak? For a moment it seemed so. But no -- it turned and walked soundlessly along the landing towards the room at the opposite end.

The young woman still watched, expecting it to speak. It was darker than ever. The doors on the upper level were all closed. Whoever...whatever...it was, it had to stop. Maybe then it would speak. It had to turn the handle...it had to open the door...and as the shaft of dim light came through, it had to turn and face her. Then she would know.

But no. The grey figure simply melted into the door and vanished. It was gone.

Young women are young women. And princess lines are princess lines. It was only after she had paraded in the kitchen, and after the dance...in fact, it wasn't till next day...that she remembered to ask the young man if anyone had left the table that night, or if anyone else was in the house.

The answer was 'no'.

The young woman married the young man, and she lived in the old house for many years. Their children slept in the room upstairs. It was now papered with embossed warriors and had blue carpet tiles on the floor. She never saw the figure again.

...Yet, she always paused at the turn in the stairs. Especially at dusk.

THE LOVELY LADY OF RICHMOND GAOL

Most of the reported ghostly 'happenings' at Richmond Gaol are what you might expect. The rattling of chains has been heard many times. Strange moans and muffled cries have sounded through the corridors. A spectral figure has been both seen and heard in the grounds and woodshed at night. Manifestations from the past come back to haunt the prison? Perhaps. A 'powerful presence' has been felt on separate occasions by a number of people, always in one particular cell. Strange? Yes. However, wouldn't it be more strange if such things were NOT felt and seen and heard in the old convict gaol?

Yet, the lovely lady of Richmond Gaol seems to have no connection with the building's convict past – unless she was the wife or relative of one of the gaol's officials. And whether she still appears in the Commandant's Quarters is not known. But the little girl, now a woman, who saw her still remembers. So does her mother.

Lucia was three years old at the time. Her mother and father had just taken over the management of the old gaol (now a tourist venue) and had moved into the former Commandant's House. It wasn't long before Lucia's mother noticed that her little girl was talking to some-one...someone who wasn't there. Always in the same room downstairs. Always in the same corner of the room.

Naturally, Lucia's mother was curious to know who the person was. "Oh, she's a lovely lady, Mummy," Lucia answered. "She's so pretty and friendly. She wears old-fashioned clothes and they're always pinky-red. She's my friend."

Of course, it is not unusual for young children to have invisible 'friends', but the curious thing is that Lucia still feels a strong presence in the house...a warm and friendly presence. She sometimes feels 'something' brush past her, particularly when she's sitting on the stairs. And she remembers very clearly the lovely lady in pinky-red.

A LADY'S GHOST – OR A GUARDIAN ANGEL?

The ghost of Gaye's Floral Boutique (Charles Street, Launceston) seems to be one for the ladies! Only females have sensed or seen his presence: Gaye (the proprietor), Loretta (her daughter), the delivery lady, a psychic friend...and others. He also seems to be something of a Guardian Angel.

Gaye first became aware of her ghost as a smell – a not- very-pleasant smell – in the room above the shop. It seemed as though something had died, but the taking up of carpets and a search of the room failed to reveal a dead rat or any other such source. The smell, which usually occurs around Christmas, St. Valentine's Day, and Mother's Day (the busiest times for a flower shop), lasts about three days. The strange thing is that if someone intrudes upstairs to smell the 'smell' – particularly a man – it disappears.

Eventually, Gaye became so intrigued and puzzled by the comings and goings of the mysterious smell that she asked her psychic friend to investigate. As soon as her friend entered the upstairs room, she felt and saw the ghostly occupant. She described him as a very large gentleman dressed in a pin stripe suit, and wearing a fob watch. "He likes you," the psychic friend added. "That's why he comes when the shop is busy. He wants to make sure everything is all right. He's a bit like a Guardian Angel."

Now, if you are somewhat sceptical about psychics (as many people are), read on. It so happens that the people who owned the building before it became Gaye's Floral Boutique have a business nearby. On being asked by Gaye about the former occupant of the upstairs room, they gave her the following information:

> The room above the shop was grandfather's. He was a large gentleman – a VERY large gentleman. He always wore a suit; and, yes, he wore a fob watch too. He used to sleep there...and, in fact, he died there.

It would seem that the very large gentleman who occupied the upstairs room – and who now makes his presence known in the form of a not-too-pleasant smell – is a Guardian Angel. Especially for the ladies.

GHOSTLY PORT ARTHUR

Port Arthur is the setting for many a ghost tale. Perhaps it is the haunted quality of the setting which explains some of the eerie happenings. Perhaps it is the work of sensitive imaginations. Perhaps...

It is easy to imagine the demented cackling of mad men as one wanders the old Lunatic Asylum. Men made crazy by long periods in solitary confinement, or separation from friends and family, or too much brutality, were incarcerated here. Some say their wild laughter can still be heard...or is it the sound of wind through the ruins?

Some say the voices of young boys can be heard at Point Puer. Boys as young as nine were sent here for crimes which today would be considered insignificant. Legend has it that two of these boys committed suicide by jumping into the sea. Some claim to have heard their screams...or was it the cry of gulls?

Some claim to have felt a ghostly presence in the Medical Officer's Quarters. Certainly a visit to the Dissection Room is a spooky experience. Situated beneath the house, it is a damp and gloomy place. Access is gained through a series of stone passages. By the time one gets there, one's imagination is already wild. Is that a blood stain on the sandstone slab? Is that faint stir of air a draught from the ventilator?

Ghostly tales surround the church. A convict with a pickaxe through his head. Another pushed to his death from the rafters. It is easy to imagine unearthly sounds and ghostly appearances inside the eyeless, roofless ruin. ...And, why IS the church unconsecrated?

Perhaps some of the ghostly stories are explained by over- stimulated imaginations ...Like the tourists who 'saw' human figures talking by the fountain at night. Figures which instantly disappeared. But the experience was so real that the group ran in terror back to their motel.

Yes, perhaps there are plausible explanations for many of the ghostly experiences at Port Arthur. But there are too many strange occurrences. Too many of those occurrences take place in the same

117

spot. Too many of them are too similar. Some of them HAVE to be 'real'.

THE MODEL PRISON

Port Arthur's Model Prison is filled with ghosts. Even in bright daylight, the suffering of those who were imprisoned seems to seep from the stone walls. Standing alone in the corridor, one can imagine the shuffling line of cowled figures as they filed into chapel, the hollow voice of a guard echoing off stone, the despairing clang of a cell door shutting...the silence.

But at night, the ghosts rise. To step through the door is to step into what seems like Hades. On either side, two rows of cells mock gapingly, their doors empty, black sockets. At the furthest end is the black hole of a fireplace surrounded by blank eyes. In the dim, flickering light, one thinks of a death mask. Was that soft footstep an echo? Or was it something else? And that sigh... What was it?

There are stories associated with the Model Prison which verify the eerie feelings. Those gaping cells seem to lure the visitor to step inside. But once in, the natural urge is to step right back out. Few humans would want to stay surrounded by those cold walls of silence and solitude. As in the case of the prisoners who were condemned to the Model Prison, only a power greater than the person could compel them stay.

That is why the happenings in cell #4 are so strange...and also why the doorway has been boarded over. The story has only been recorded twice, but the occasions are so similar in detail, and so compelling, that the cell has been made out of bounds. In the words of tour guide, Patricia, "People get frozen in there."

In both cases, the people who had stepped inside to view cell #4 found themselves trapped – not because the door had closed, but because SOMETHING had made them powerless. And that 'something' was a terrifying thing...a horrifying 'someone'. Not only were they powerless to step outside, they were powerless to move or speak. Both individuals were found in the same corner. Both were in the foetal position. Both were rigid with terror. Both had to be literally carried out of the cell and away from the prison.

But that is not the end of cell #4

119

It is the belief of some that tampering with the stones of old buildings releases the spirits. Perhaps this explains the following story: A restoration crew had been engaged to work on the Model Prison. The workers were taking a break from their task of repairing some of the cells. The group had gathered around their leader, who was leaning against the wall of the corridor – right next to the doorway of cell #4. A few jokes were made. A few directions were given. The workers were just being like workers on their mid morning break... When, suddenly, the group leader felt someone...or something...grab his arm. Not just grab; it was a clutch. A HARD clutch! Looking around, he saw that the muscular arm came from the door of cell #4! And he had the bruises to prove it!

If cell #4 doesn't provide quite enough in the way of ghostly stories, there is the deaf and dumb cell. Recalcitrant prisoners were placed here for what must have been the most terrifying punishment of all. Not a ray of light pierces the darkness; not a sound penetrates the maze of stone walls. Here the prisoner was kept for up to three days. Some emerged raving mad. Today, as they experience their three minutes of darkness, some visitors report hearing sighs and moans. The work of sensitive imaginations? ...Or the muted spirits of men caught in stone?

And perhaps it is the anger of those muted spirits which accounts for the cameras that won't work, and the flashlights that go out.

Yes, Port Arthur's Model Prison is filled with ghosts.

The Ghosts of Entally House
The clockface which opens.

Model Prison, Port Arthur
The haunted cell.

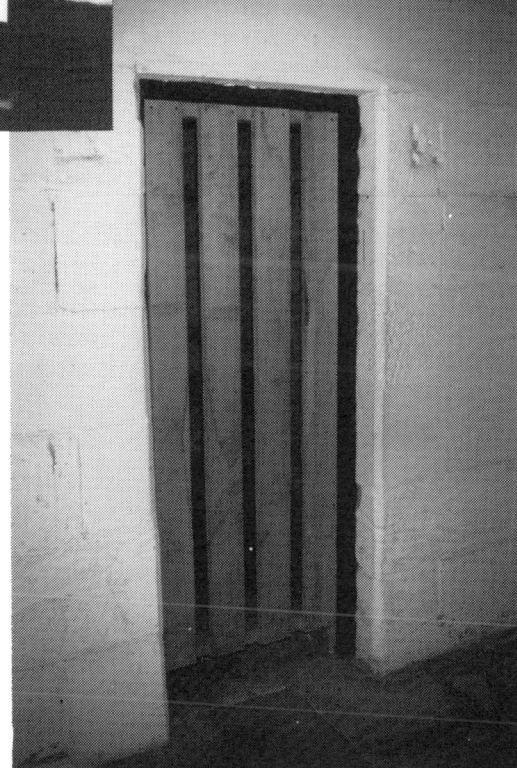

THE PARSON'S HOUSE

The sounds of children playing. A gentleman sitting by the fire. A ghostly grey lady with a lamp. These are all part of the haunted nature of the Parson's House. But there is something sinister...something ominous...something terrifying about the old cottage.

To the casual passerby, the Parson's House looks harmless enough. It is one of a row of 'official' residences overlooking the penal settlement of Port Arthur. Having witnessed so much of the former prison's sad history, the cottage SHOULD be haunted. And, by most reports, it IS. However, in view of the history of which it is part, the laughter of children is not the phenomenon one might expect.

Yet, the Parson's house was a normal home – or as normal as a home could be in such abnormal circumstances. Families lived here, and children played. It seems that some of that laughter still sounds from time to time, sometimes in the attic, sometimes in the garden.

Patricia has heard the childish sounds a number of times. Alone in the house, she has searched for the children who may have entered. But the attic was empty, with no signs of play. Nor were there children to be seen outside.

Patricia (and others) – again while alone in the house – has heard the tread of heavy, booted feet on the stairs. Also the sound of a fire crackling...when there was no fire. One attendant, who went to investigate the unexpected sound, surprised a ghostly apparition sitting in the fireside chair. As the door opened, the figure vanished.

Then there are the reports of the grey lady who is said to wander the house at night. Carrying the lamp, she roams the corridors and stairs – soundlessly. One account (from the days when the Parson's House was still a residence) tells of her entering the room where a visitor had just put her baby to sleep. The grey lady stepped silently to the crib; then stood for a few moments, looking down at the child. She then stooped to kiss the sleeping infant.

When the mother asked about the lady in grey who carried the lamp and kissed her baby, she was told there was no such person in the house.

To this point, the ghostly presences of the Parson's House seem harmless enough (if somewhat unusual). But it is the experience of a restoration worker which throws an ominous complexion on its haunted nature. The young man, who lived in Hobart, was using the Parson's House as overnight accommodation.

It was during the third night that the terrifying occurrence took place. Telling himself that the experiences of the first two nights – the eerie sounds, and the feeling of something 'pressing down' as he tried to sleep – were figments of his imagination, he settled down in his sleeping bag on the floor. How long he had been there he could not say. What he does remember is being suddenly jerked out of sleep by the unmistakable feeling of hands at his throat. Strong hands. Gripping. Choking. Something – someone – was trying to strangle him! It was more than a dream, as the bruises next day were to prove.

The young man never did sleep in the Parson's House again. Perhaps (as in the case of the Model Prison) the restoration work had disturbed resentful spirits. Likewise, tourists sometimes report cameras and torches which refuse to work.

These days, no one spends the night in the Parson's House. Laughter and footsteps seem harmless enough, but there is something eerie about the old house at night. It is as though locked windows and closed doors hold back a host of unhappy demons.

Yes, there is something sinister about the Parson's House. Something ominous. Something terrifying. Something not quite nice.

THE COMMANDANT'S HOUSE

As one looks down onto the ruins of the old penal settlement of Port Arthur, it is impossible to be unaware of the haunted quality of the place. The beauty of the setting contrasts uncompromisingly with the stark outlines of the penitentiary, the lunatic asylum, the model prison...with the Isle of the Dead and Point Puer beyond.

The Commandant's House may seem isolated from it all – but is it? Even casual tourists are aware of the eeriness of that substantial dwelling, once occupied by the notorious O'Hara Booth, and which stands slightly apart from the prison complex. And some have hard evidence of a phenomena that is hard to explain!

Caretakers of the Commandant's House report perplexing occurrences...like the gate which opens by itself...and a window which seems to like to be sky-high. Their last duty of the day is to secure all doors and windows, yet many times early-morning workers have arrived to find the window wide.

The front bedroom also holds its mysteries. Patricia, one of Port Arthur's tour guides, has her own story. The room was the sleeping place of former Commandant, O'Hara Booth. His bed is kept meticulously made and smooth. It is also roped off from the public. Yet Patricia speaks of the occasions when she has found the imprint of a large body on the bed. Yet, after she has smoothed out the covers, the shape reappears.

Patricia also tells of the sound of footsteps, and the sound of someone reading. And someone rocking.

The rocking chair is in the room at the end and to the left of the long corridor. It is a simple colonial chair which stands in the corner. Of course, one's imagination has already been fired as one passes through the shadowy passage with glimpses into mysterious, old-world rooms...but the chair looks innocent enough. Yet, on occasions when the Commandant's House has been empty, the distinct sound of rocking has frequently been heard. Some have even discovered the chair to be moving...as though an occupant has just disappeared.

Also puzzling are the times tourists' cameras won't work when their owners try to take pictures of the haunted rocking chair.

...But strangest of all are the are the pictures which DO work. They frequently show weird, wraith-like shapes. And sometimes the shape of a woman. Rocking.

The Bare Bones of Fred
Theatre boxes.

The Powder Magazine,
Port Arthur
Sentry box.

THE POWDER MAGAZINE

Like the other ruins of Port Arthur, the Powder Magazine SHOULD be haunted. And, of course, it is (or so they say).

Sounds of footsteps pacing. Moans of anguish. Cries of protested innocence. These phenomena should not be surprising, for the Powder Magazine was not used for storage only. It was also a lookout point for sentries, and, at one time, it was the condemned cell.

The story goes that a young man was sentenced to hang, and was awaiting transportation to Hobart Town and the gallows. As the appointed day of his departure drew closer, his anguished cries of innocence grew louder and louder...until they filled the settlement and penetrated each stone cell.

No one could escape those tormented sounds, least of all the guards who paced overhead. And, apparently, they still pace.